DATE DUE

The Laughter
at the
Heart of Things

SELECTED ESSAYS

The Laughter
at the
Heart of Things

SELECTED ESSAYS

HELEN M. LUKE

PARABOLA BOOKS

NEW YORK

Published by
Parabola Books
656 Broadway
New York, NY 10012

2|06

website: www.parabola.org

Library of Congress Cataloging-in-Publication Data
Luke, Helen M., 1904–
    The laughter at the heart of things : selected essays / by Helen M. Luke.
— 1st ed.
128 p. cm.
    Contents: Drama: The ring. Reflections on Shakespeare (The merchant of
Venice, Antony and Cleopatra). Oresteia — Musings: The stranger within.
Jacob and Esau. The laughter at the heart of things. Goddess of the hearth.
    ISBN 0-930407-52-0 (alk. paper)
    1. Literature — History and criticism. I. Title.

PN511.L78 2001
809—dc21   2001021667

The paper used in this publication meets the minimum requirements of the
American National Standard for Permanence of Paper for Printed Library
Materials Z39.48-1984

Book design by Studio 31

Printed in the United States of America

Excerpts from "The Story of Baucis and Philemon" in Ovid, *Metamorphoses,*
translated by Rolf Humphries, were reprinted by permission of Indiana University Press.

CONTENTS

FOREWORD BY PETER BROOK   7

PART ONE: DRAMA   9

THE RING   10

REFLECTIONS ON SHAKESPEARE   37

The Merchant of Venice   41

Antony and Cleopatra   59

PART TWO: MUSINGS   89

ORESTEIA: AN EYE FOR AN EYE   90

THE STRANGER WITHIN   96

JACOB AND ESAU   104

THE LAUGHTER AT THE HEART OF THINGS   107

GODDESS OF THE HEARTH   119

NOTES   127

FOREWORD

I first read Helen Luke because a great friend of mine in London, who often draws my attention to something very interesting in a book, said, "Have you read *Old Age* by Helen Luke?" I said no. He said, "You are preparing *The Tempest*. There's something about *The Tempest* in there. You must read it." And the moment I read this book, the impression was of something that goes far beyond words, ideas, theories, philosophies, all of which, for me, have no meaning at all. I don't think there is a single word in the vocabulary that has any meaning if you separate it from the feeling that gives it life. And ever since, everything I have read of Helen Luke and the words we've exchanged on the telephone are informed with a particular quality, and that quality is so fine, so sensitive, so warm, and so close to a very deep and true source, that naturally the feeling is one of closeness.

Since then, I've come to know the objective facts about Luke's work as a young Jungian, the range of her studies, the nature of her interests, the community that has developed around her. Instead of meeting her from the outside, as happens most times in life, when you gradually begin to get to know a person better until the point where you decide the person is either very remarkable or not as interesting as you thought at first, here it was quite the other way round. My first "meeting" with Luke was so essential that the rest fell into place around it.

Life is a mysterious, terrifying, powerful, and wondrous unfolding experience. I think Helen Luke is firmly there, an acutely perceptive person who picked up and sustained ancient truths, which naturally go against the frequently destructive and chaotic nature of contemporary life. One has to be not only grateful for this, but very attentive to this quality. Most of all, it is important to remember that ideas mean nothing, and that any theory whatsoever that isn't at the same time sustained by a living experience isn't worth the paper it's written on. Luke's ideas are expressions of what she lived and what she became.

There are prophets, there are guides, and there are argumentative people with theories, and one must be careful to discriminate between them. In our time, there have been certain people whose research has brought them above the level of argumentation, with a new theory— they have opened up dark ideas, thrown light onto them, and permitted new questions to arise. But none of them knows the whole secret, the whole mystery of human existence. So we mustn't quarrel over who was the greater, but recognize that all men are unequal, born unequal in an inner genetic way, and that through the way they live their lives they develop unequally. There are people who manage, through their own efforts and through great help, to become "remarkable men," as they are called in the film of G. I. Gurdjieff's book, *Meetings with Remarkable Men*. Of course, "remarkable men" also means "remarkable women," and I can't think of a better example today of a remarkable man in that sense than Helen Luke.

—Peter Brook

PART ONE

DRAMA

The Ring

A living myth is told and retold as the centuries pass. Poets, painters, musicians are nourished by its imagery, and in each retelling something is added from the collective attitudes, conscious and unconscious, of the time and from the individual vision of the artist. In the nineteenth century Richard Wagner was inspired by the legend of Siegfried and the ring to write his four great musical dramas: *The Rhinegold, The Valkyrie, Siegfried,* and *The Twilight of the Gods,* calling the whole cycle *The Ring of the Nibelungen.* The complete work was first performed in 1876. Some seventy to eighty years later, in our own times, another Ring cycle was published by a great artist, having its sources in the same myth of the ring of absolute power—*The Lord of the Rings* by J. R. R. Tolkien.

It is of great interest to compare the likenesses and differences between these two eruptions of the ring symbol in the nineteenth century and in our own time. For example, in both stories the ring emerges from the unconscious into this world, promising absolute power to its possessor, bearing a curse which breeds violence, deceit, and corruption of heart and mind. "Care shall consume the ones who possess it and envy gnaw those who wish that they did. Each shall lust after its delights yet no one shall find any profit. Let death be his portion, fear be the bread he eats!" These words of Alberich's curse apply in every detail to the nature of the ring of Sauron: "One ring to bring them all and in the darkness bind them." In both cycles the whole world is in jeopardy unless the ring can be returned to its source by a human being; and in both the redemption is followed by the death of the gods, or, in the symbolism of Tolkien, by the departure from this world of the numinous, of elf and wizard.

The differences are equally fascinating. In the German myth Siegfried is entirely unconscious of the ring's meaning and of his task; even Brunhilde only breaks through to some awareness of what it is all about after Siegfried has been murdered. Frodo, on the contrary, takes up the burden of the ringbearer consciously, of his own free will, in full knowledge of the dangers and temptations involved in his quest. Brunhilde returns the ring to the water maidens; Frodo returns it to the fire. The fire in *The Twilight of the Gods* consumes hero and heroine, their horse, and the gods, as well as Hagen, son of Alberich. The fire of Mount Doom destroys the ring, Gollum, all the structures of the Dark Lord, and Frodo's ring finger; and the "gods" withdraw sadly but willingly from the earth when the time is ripe. To the meaning of these things we will return later after discussing *The Ring of the Nibelungen* cycle in some detail. Whereas Tolkien's story is well-known to most of us, Wagner's version of the myth is probably familiar only to the musicians among us. We shall therefore begin with a summary of the four librettos of his Ring operas.

THE STORY

The Rhinegold

The Rhinegold opens with a scene in the depths of the river where the Rhine maidens guard the Rhinegold. Alberich, an ugly dwarf of the Nibelungen race emerges from a cave and watches the maidens at play, lusting after their beauty. They tease and mock him and he tries to catch one of them, his anger and desire growing stronger as they elude him. Then suddenly a golden light shines through the water, the gleaming of the Rhinegold, and Alberich, startled, questions the maidens, who tell him that if anyone could fashion a ring out of this gold he would be able to rule the world—nothing could stand against his power. That is why they guard it so carefully. They then reveal that only he who forswears all the joys of love can forge the ring from the gold, and say contemptuously to each other that for this reason they need have no fear of this dwarf who is panting with lust.

Alberich, however, is possessed immediately by a greed for power more than compensating for the loss of everything else and speaks to the nymphs: "Make love in the darkness, fishified race—hear this, O waves! I renounce love and curse it." And so he bears the gold from the rock and leaves the maidens crying "Woe!" in the darkness.

Meanwhile, Wotan is sitting on the mountaintop above the Rhine, gloating over the beauty of his new castle of Valhalla, which has been built for him by the giants. Fricka, his wife, reminds him of the terrible price which must be paid, for Wotan had thoughtlessly promised to give Freia to the giants in return for their work—Freia, the goddess of youth and of all growing things, she who grows the golden apples by which alone the gods are kept alive. Fricka chides Wotan for his hardhearted greed for power which had led him to make so wicked a promise. He reminds her that she, too, longed for the building of Valhalla so that she could keep him at home and check his wanderings.

Fasolt and Fafnir, the giants, come to claim their wages. Wotan calls desperately on Loki for help. Loki is the god of fire, the god of cunning tricks and dark riddles. He says that the only way to save Freia is to offer the giants something they would desire more than the love of woman, and then he tells of Alberich's theft of the gold and his forging of the ring of power. Both Wotan and the giants immediately begin to covet it, and the giants go off with Freia, saying they will hold her as hostage until Wotan can steal the ring from Alberich and give it to them as ransom.

We now see Alberich beating and tormenting his brother Mime, a master smith of the dwarves, all of whom Alberich has now enslaved to his will through the ring. Mime, following careful instructions from Alberich, has just made for him a helm, the Tarnhelm, which makes its wearer invisible and can transform him into any shape he wills. Wotan and Loki arrive to find Mime alone and cowering, and he tells them of the ring and of the helmet and of how Alberich has forced the dwarves to mine a huge hoard of treasure for him. Alberich arrives, the Tarnhelm hanging from his belt, and begins boasting to the gods of his wealth and of how he will eventually emerge from under the earth to the light of day, and all men and gods will fall under the spell of gold and will forswear all other loves, and the world will belong to him, Alberich, to do with as he wills. Playing on his vanity, Loki now tricks Alberich into showing the power of the Tarnhelm. Cunningly he lures him on until the dwarf turns himself into a toad, whereupon Loki and Wotan capture the toad, remove the Tarnhelm, and bind Alberich. They then demand his hoard and his ring in return for his life. Alberich desperately tries to keep the ring, but when it is torn from him he curses all who will carry it.

Fasolt and Fafnir come with Freia to exchange her for the gold, and Wotan, like Alberich, tries to hold back the ring. But the giants pile up the treasure round Freia until she is hidden save for one chink, which the ring will close. They refuse to release her until she is completely invisible to them—that is, until love is completely buried in gold. Wotan gives in, but only after Erda, the Earth Mother herself, has risen up to warn him of the fearful consequences of keeping it. The giants immediately start quarreling as to which of them will take the ring, and Fafnir kills Fasolt. This is the first death of the curse.

The gods now pass over the rainbow bridge to their glorious new castle of Valhalla, and the Rhine maidens are heard mourning for their gold. Wotan curses them for their harrowing noise.

The Valkyrie

The attempts of the upper and the lower powers to hold the ring have failed. The giant guards it in the form of a dragon, and only a human hero who knows no fear can contend with him. So we are now told the story of the events leading to the birth of this hero, Siegfried.

Sieglinda (Siegfried's mother-to-be) is married to Hunding, but one evening her unrecognized twin brother Siegmund comes to her dwelling and they fall deeply in love. Siegmund now finds the sword Nothung, which his father, Wotan, had left for him sticking in the ash tree which grows in Hunding's house. Only he can draw it out. He and Sieglinda flee together, Siegfried is conceived, and there is war between Siegmund and Hunding. Wotan, who had begotten Siegmund and Sieglinda on a mortal woman, loves his son and would befriend him, but Fricka, the outraged goddess of marriage, forces him to promise that Siegmund shall die and Hunding be victorious. Wotan had longed to create a free man but had failed.

So now, despite himself, he must kill his beloved son who had defied law—and the agent of this must be his own daughter Brunhilde. She is the chief of the Valkyrie, the warrior maidens, whose task is to bring dead heroes from the battlefield to live with the gods and protect them. Perceiving that Wotan's order is not his true desire, she plans to spare Siegmund and let him kill Hunding. Wotan, in fury at her disobedience, comes himself to the battle. Nothung is shattered against his spear and Siegmund dies. Brunhilde, however, overcome with pity, carries off Sieglinda to safety, and then must face the wrath of her father. She is condemned to sleep on a rock encircled by fire from which she can only be released by the kiss of a mortal man. She is somewhat comforted by the thought that only a hero without fear could penetrate the flames. Wotan now takes on the guise of the Wanderer and goes out into the world.

Siegfried

Sieglinda has found refuge in the cave of Mime, the dwarf smith, brother of Alberich, and she dies giving birth to Siegfried. The child is brought up by Mime in the hope that the boy, when grown, will kill the dragon Fafnir for him so that he can get his hands on the treasure and the ring. As Siegfried grows to manhood Mime forges sword after sword for him, but each one the boy breaks as soon as it is made, abusing his foster-father, whom he treats with extreme contempt and loathing, while Mime harps continually on all his seeming kindness to the boy. Finally Siegfried, having noticed that all birds and animals have mothers, forces Mime to tell him of his own mother, and out comes the story of his father's broken sword, the pieces of which Sieglinda had brought with her to the cave. Siegfried orders him to weld the sword together and storms out. There follows the arrival of Wotan, disguised as the Wanderer, who tells the dwarf that only Siegfried, the boy who knows no fear, can reforge the sword.

On Siegfried's return, Mime resolves to teach him fear and gain power over him that way. Siegfried is quite undismayed by the gruesome pictures Mime conjures up but is nevertheless most anxious to learn what that strange thing "fear" is. So when Mime tells him he can learn it from the dragon Fafnir, he is eager to be off and, seizing the pieces of the sword Nothung, reforges them himself and splits the anvil in half with the newly welded blade.

At the dragon's cave there is a confrontation between Wotan and Alberich, who spends his time watching there, hoping to regain the ring. The subhuman and the superhuman late possessors of the ring stand before the dragon's cave, but Wotan knows, as Alberich does not, that only the human hero can wrest the ring from the dragon now. He warns Alberich of Siegfried's approach with the plotting Mime.

Siegfried, waiting under a tree for the dragon to emerge, dreams of his father and mother and hears a forest bird singing. He wishes he could understand the language of the bird. Then Fafnir arrives, and Siegfried demands to be taught fear. They defy each other and Siegfried plunges Nothung into the dragon's heart, and as he draws it out his hand is splashed with blood, which burns like fire. Siegfried sucks his hand and so drinks a little of the dragon's poison, and his ears are opened so that he can now understand the language of the birds. The forest bird then tells him to take the ring and the Tarnhelm from the hoard and also not to trust Mime, who now appears with a drink for the tired warrior, which he has poisoned. Siegfried refuses to drink and kills Mime. Then he speaks to the bird of his loneliness and learns of Brunhilde, whom only a hero without fear can rescue from her living death within the flaming circle. Eagerly he sets off to find her, to learn fear from her.

On the way he meets the Wanderer, Wotan, who has just been telling the Earth Mother, Erda, that the rule of the gods will soon be over and that the world will be redeemed by a man who wins the ring. Nevertheless, as is his way, he now tries to prevent Siegfried from reaching Brunhilde, since it will mean the fall of the gods. Siegfried, shouting insults as usual, breaks Wotan's spear with Nothung and goes on his way. Then he walks through the fire and thinks at first, seeing her armor, that Brunhilde is a man. When he recognizes her as a woman, he kisses her and she awakes. He is ardently and passionately in love, but at first she rejects him in great fear, for to respond will mean loss of her divinity. Now it is his turn to realize that he may lose her, and so he knows fear at last. He continues to woo her and she finally yields, her own passion overwhelming her. They swear eternal love and pass the night in the cave, and in the morning Siegfried goes off to perform heroic deeds, giving Brunhilde the ring as pledge of his love.

The Twilight of the Gods

Brunhilde, left alone, is visited by one of her Valkyrie sisters who urges her to return the ring to the Rhine maidens as the only way of saving the gods and the world. Brunhilde refuses with a contemptuous laugh. Nothing in heaven or earth could make her part with Siegfried's gift.

Meanwhile, Siegfried comes to the Rhine and to a castle where he meets Gunther and his sister Gutrune and his half-brother Hagen, the son of Alberich. Hagen determines to get the ring from Siegfried, urged on by Alberich. He persuades Gunther and Gutrune to give the hero a magic potion, which makes him forget all about Brunhilde and fall in

love immediately with Gutrune. Gunther has long had a dream of mar-
rying Brunhilde but knows he has no hope of winning her, and Siegfried
offers to go in Gunther's shape, through the power of the Tarnhelm, and
win Brunhilde for him. So they set off and Siegfried, as Gunther, again
penetrates the fire and claims Brunhilde, taking the ring from her as she
calls on its power. Protesting in terrible grief, she is led to the castle by
the Rhine where she finds Siegfried unfaithful and discovers his trick. In
her rage she tells Hagen that she has made Siegfried invulnerable except
in the back, thus sending Siegfried to his death.

Siegfried, having sworn blood brotherhood with Gunther, goes
hunting with him and Hagen. Alone for a while beside the Rhine, he
sees the Rhine maidens rise from the water and they beg him to return
the ring, flattering him. He refuses. They disappear and he hesitates,
thinking that he might give it freely—that he would like to possess one
of them, if he were not true to Gutrune. Now they return and this time
they threaten him, telling him of the ring's curse and how he will be
killed if he doesn't part with it. This simply makes him start boasting
again of how he isn't afraid of anything, and he refuses finally to give it
up.

Hagen and the others arrive and question him about his reputed
power to understand the speech of birds. He replies, "It is long since I
heeded their chatter—since I heard women singing I have quite forgotten the birds." He tells the story of his life, and after a drink prepared by
Hagen his memory is fully restored and he remembers Brunhilde and
his love. Hagen then stabs him in the back. Singing of Brunhilde rising
for the second time from sleep, he dies greeting her.

Siegfried's body is carried back to the castle—to Gutrune and Brunhilde. Hagen now tries to take the ring from Siegfried's finger, but the
dead hand is raised and checks him. Brunhilde orders a great funeral
pyre to be raised that she and his horse, Grane, may join him in the
flames. She sings now of her love of the great hero, who, truest of all,
was forced to betray her that she might finally learn wisdom; then she
speaks to her father, sending home his ravens with the news "both feared
and longed for"—the end of the gods.

Drawing the ring from Siegfried's finger, and calling on the Rhine
maidens to claim it from the ashes, Brunhilde cries, "May the fire that
burns me cleanse the ring from its curse! Dissolve it in the stream and
ever keep safe the pure shining gold whose theft wrought such evil!"

She throws a flaming brand into the pyre and speaks to Grane, her horse and Siegfried's, "My friend, do you know whither I lead you—are you neighing to follow your friend?" Joyfully she mounts and together they plunge into the fire. The Rhine rises, and on the flood come the Rhine maidens who hold up the ring, which Brunhilde has flung to them. In the heavens Valhalla and all the gods within it are consumed in the flames.

THE COMMENTARY

Wagner begins by making clear the origin and the nature of the ring of power. It is forged from the gold hidden in the depths of the unconscious, where there is no differentiation of good and evil. This gold, this treasure, lies in the womb of the great mother; her daughters, the Rhine maidens, collective anima figures of man's psyche, play and disport themselves around it, basking in the light of its beauty. They are its guardians, and from them it must be stolen if it is to reach the light of day, emerge into consciousness. In every age some individuals have dared consciously to descend and to take this gold, forging it into the circle of wholeness, of the Self, but for the most part it is stolen by the collective shadow of mankind, of which Alberich is the symbol. By him it is also forged into a symbol of the totality, but through his denial of Eros or love it becomes a small and exclusive ring, which may be used and possessed only by its owner. Just as the individual, singly not collectively, may come to wholeness only when he has found that to be finally alone is to include all, so one man alone can possess the ring of Alberich, identifying the totality with his personal will to power and excluding all that is other.

In *The Lord of the Rings,* as in the *Nibelungen* cycle, it is stressed that only one man at a time can wield the power of the ring. It is a symbolic statement of the truth that we cannot ever seek refuge from individual responsibility by blaming collective forces—that salvation and damnation alike are encountered by each man alone. The circle of wholeness and the ring of Alberich and Sauron are basically one and the same—the positive and negative poles of the Self. That which determines the nature of the power bestowed by the ring is the degree of consciousness with which each and every one of us responds to that love which is both "center and circumference." He who has reached the stage of "Love and do what you will" is completely free from any temptation whatsoever to *use* the ring whether for good or evil purpose, whereas he who rejects love and does what he wills is delivered over to possession by the ring, and so to ultimate destruction. For if *The Rhinegold,* indeed if the whole cycle makes anything clear, it is above all this—that the finding of the gold, the ring's forging, its passage from hand to hand, and the manner of the curse's operation on everyone who carries it or covets it are all determined by the individual's relationship to Eros, and to the meaning of love.

At the outset the gold is in the possession of the anima, of the unconscious, feminine principle in man. Alberich finds it when he is moved by lust of the lowest kind, but nevertheless the object of his lust is the beauty of the Rhine maidens. Through it he glimpses the beauty of the gold in the unconscious and through it he learns that the ring can only be forged at all by a man who has renounced love. This is true both of the ring of world domination *and* of the circle of wholeness, though in opposite senses. The seeker after the truth of love, just as the seeker after personal power, can only find the gold at all through the experience of his passionate, instinctive nature, and from this experience he learns that when his desire is purged of all possessiveness, all demand, he will be able to forge the ring of wholeness. For him this purging of Eros is the way to that love which is beyond desire, the love of which Jung is speaking when he says that only when a man can renounce any and every desire without a moment's hesitation has he found the Self. Nevertheless, only *through* desire can desire be transcended.

For Alberich, on the other hand, the renunciation of love means the total rejection of all the feminine values of relationship, of all tenderness and kindness, of all respect for the individual—a total exclusion of all but his own will. In Tolkien's story the ring has been forged long before the book opens, but Sauron is plainly the symbol of the complete denial of every kind of human relatedness. In his country there came a slow death to every growing thing. Eros being cast out, not even a plant could propagate.

In our own time we see this murder of Eros values on every side. It reveals itself in the deification of the collective "good," so-called, and the justification of every conceivable horror in its service—and not only in Nazi and Communist countries, as people so often comfortably assume.

The energy of Eros, repressed and rejected, is turned invariably, in small matters as in great, into the insatiable pursuit of power, whereas its full acceptance and transformation through conscious sacrifice of the ego will give birth to the power of that love which is perfect freedom from desire. We have only to look about us and into our own hearts. Wherever we see a demand that things should go our own way, whenever we try to push people into behaving in the way we imagine to be right, we are forcing the Eros gold into a ring of personal exclusive power.

All this is not surprising because at bottom love *is* power. There is a Zen story which shows that if a sage is watching a stream flowing or a pebble falling he has *commanded* the water to flow or the stone to fall. How so? Because since it *is* so he has willed it to be so—or rather his will and every conceivable fact are one thing. It is not at all the same thing as a mere acquiescence or resigned acceptance; it is absolute power never used for any end, and the negative side of this total love is the absolute power of destruction, which comes to him who has entirely refused Eros and whose ego is therefore inflated to the point where the whole universe exists to serve its will.

There is another interesting parallel between the two stories in the theme of invisibility. As soon as the ring of Sauron is put on it makes its wearer invisible, and in the *Nibelungen* story Alberich causes the Tarnhelm, which brings invisibility, to be forged at the same time as the ring. The substitution of power for love makes a man invisible to others—he no longer exists as a distinct person.

While Alberich was renouncing Eros and forging the ring under the earth, Wotan, the god in the sky, was in a semiconscious way also busy betraying the values of the heart in the service of his own pride. He had employed the giants to build Valhalla for him, a magnificent palace and stronghold, and he had bribed them with an infamous promise. A vast structure of self-glorification in consciousness parallels the similar process down below. The giants symbolize Wotan's own inflated idea of himself, and an inflation, if indulged in and used to enhance personal glory or safety, exacts precisely the price that Wotan had undertaken to pay—that is, the goddess Freia, she whose golden apples are the only food that could keep him alive at all. Every inflation is followed by depression, apathy, and loss of energy, a failure of the life-giving food of the goddess, the nourishment that comes to man through human relationship. Wotan, like Alberich, had promised to give up Eros, but unlike

Alberich, he is ashamed of his promise and wants to get out of it. He is the ruling principle of consciousness in the myth, and he wants to have his cake and eat it too. He made the promise without facing the fact that he might really have to fulfill it one day, trusting in the god Loki (the trickster, the Lucifer of the myth) to find a way out when the time came. How familiar this sounds! Indeed, all the ambivalent goings-on of Wotan are immediately recognizable as a picture of the self-deceptions, the generosities and meannesses, the nobility and cowardice, that live side by side in us all.

The giants are coming to claim the goddess. Loki has produced as yet no solution, and that other goddess, Fricka, Wotan's wife, the protector of marriage and respectability, upbraids Wotan for his betrayal of Freia. He protests, however, that she was as anxious as he to build the castle, in order to keep him at home with her. When a ruling principle is dying, feeling regresses into possessiveness and conventionality. It will be seen later how Fricka undermines and almost destroys Wotan's true feeling, symbolized by Brunhilde.

The giants demand immediate payment, Freia appeals desperately to Wotan, and now Loki appears with his solution. The giants must be offered something they will value more highly than the goddess, so that they will freely give up their claim to her. It must be remembered that there is one sin Wotan cannot commit without losing his power forever. He cannot break his given word. His spear is the symbol of his rulership of the world and on it are graven all the solemn vows that he makes. If ever he is untrue to such a vow, he knows that the spear will break in pieces and his power be shattered. It is indeed true that if the ruling principle of consciousness betrays its own nature, its "word" in this basic sense, it must inevitably crumble—we do not trust it any more and so its power to rule is gone. So Wotan can plan every kind of trick except this one, and Loki, his shadow, must find a way out without risking this betrayal.

Loki now tells of the ring of power that Alberich has forged. If Wotan can obtain this ring and give it to the giants, they will relinquish Freia. It is an irony that in order to keep his word, and with it his world domination, he must give into the hands of the giants the ring that will give them precisely that same power which he is trying (with one side of himself) to save. Wotan, however, is not an Alberich. He will not at the last betray Eros for the sake of power, and finally, with great reluctance, he hands the ring to the giants.

Thus the ring, taken from Alberich by a trick, is brought up from the underworld into the light of day and passes into the hands of the giants, who in their turn have renounced Eros, their lusting after Freia, in order to obtain it. The curse is immediately demonstrated. Only one man can wear it, and all who have turned their backs on love must covet it. Fasolt and Fafnir fight, and Fasolt is killed. But Fafnir is stupid. He has immense physical strength and the devouring greed of instinct, but he is incapable of using the ring. So the ring possesses him, and he regresses into the form of a dragon, buries the treasure and the ring in a cave, and spends his life hanging onto it. We are reminded of Gollum in the later story doing the same thing—sitting in the darkness under the mountain, alone with his devouring passion for "his precious," for the ring. He too, like Fafnir, had committed murder to gain it and had not enough conscious strength to use it, and so the ring gradually devours what little humanity remains in either of them, shutting them away from all relationship in a terrible loneliness. This is what happens to all of us to the extent that we *hide* not only from others but from ourselves the secret desires for power, which can take on so many subtle disguises.

It is a situation, however, that cannot last, and so in both the Wagner and the Tolkien stories the ring is at last brought out into the open by a human being of good will into whose hands passes the fate of the world. Siegfried defeats the dragon and takes the ring for his own; Bilbo defeats Gollum in a battle of words; but neither the hobbit nor the hero is aware of the meaning of the ring. Each carries it lightheartedly, and they are both for some time protected from its curse because of their fundamental good will—Siegfried is finally destroyed by it because he refuses to give it up; Bilbo is saved because he relinquishes it of his own free will.

Both Siegfried and Bilbo in effect *steal* the ring, as Alberich stole it from the Rhine maidens, Fafnir from Fasolt, and as Gollum stole it from his friend who found it in the river, and before him Isildur from Sauron himself. Theft is a widespread motif in myth. Hermes is a thief as well as a guide. Prometheus stole the fire from Heaven. Consciousness is, as it were, stolen from the unconscious, and it is only when we have dared to *steal* that we have the experience of grace—of that which is freely given, unearned and unsought. Does it perhaps mean that the ego *must* dare to assert itself even in face of all the transcendent powers of conscious and unconscious, *must* take to itself the ring of power, identifying in a moment of extreme danger even with the totality of the Self, before the miracle of grace can happen which frees a man forever from desire and possessiveness?

When Frodo puts on the ring on the edge of Mount Doom, it is not *only* a falling before the deadly power of the thing he has carried for so long, it is also a divine theft, a tremendous assertion of himself: "I, Frodo, will keep and wield this power." If this assertion had been made *before* the long purging of his journey and before his victorious battle with the temptations of power, he and the world with him would have been utterly destroyed. But the assertion of his ego at this last crucial moment is somehow, we feel—though we can make no rational explanation of it—a condition of the final release through the miracles of Gollum's saving act and of the coming of the Eagles. Must each man be able to say I *am* the Self, before he can know that he both is and is not? Exactly the same truth is behind Psyche's theft at the last and crucial moment of the beauty of Persephone from the box she carries, and her rescue by Eros himself. It is the timing, the *unpremeditated* timing of such a theft, that is crucial. These are ultimately thefts, but each small growth in consciousness is likewise a theft, followed, *if* it is made at the right time, by an immediate letting go. We cannot let go of something we have not made our own. Only when Milarepa, the great Tibetan sage, as a young man, became exasperated with his guru who kept putting off the moment of beginning to teach him the secret doctrine and *stole* the holy books did his guru know was ready to learn. "The kingdom of heaven suffereth violence and the violent take it by force." A man must be able to say, "I will have, I will *take* this thing for myself," before he can discover that it can never be taken, only given. Only through desire are we freed from desire.

To return now to the story: At the end of *The Rhinegold*, the ring, stolen by the collective shadow from the feminine waters, stolen by Wotan, by collective consciousness, from the shadow, has been taken by what we may call the personal unconscious and is lying dormant awaiting a human ego who will have the courage to seize it. The giants are personal shadow figures of the gods. (Gollum is the shadow of Bilbo, Frodo, Sam—of each and every hobbit.) Meanwhile the Rhine maidens in the depths are lamenting their loss, asserting that all truth lies down there—while Wotan with the gods retreats into his remote castle in the air and curses the horrible noises the unconscious is making! It is a stalemate, a state of high tension—the opposites split wide apart and the ring that unites them for good or ill lying hidden in the cave. "One ring to bring them all and in the darkness bind them," as Tolkien writes—or, we might add, one ring to bring freedom and love through the total sacrifice of power.

The second drama of the cycle, *The Valkyrie,* tells the story of the meeting of Siegfried's father and mother, of the hero and his near-destruction before birth; it shows also the beginning of the equally long and hazardous preparation of the heroine, of the anima figure, immortal daughter of Wotan, for her task of awakening Siegfried to fear and to love, so that he may likewise awaken her from sleep to the acceptance of mortality and death.

Siegmund and Seiglinda were begotten by Wotan on a mortal woman in an attempt to create a man who will defy the gods—who will become a whole and free individual no longer bound to project his unconscious onto gods and devils. Here we see the double nature of the unconscious at its most profound—for the urge to wholeness, which is constantly pushing us towards consciousness, is balanced by the immensely strong pull backwards into inertia and darkness. Wotan demonstrates this ambivalence at his every appearance in the story. Human parents, insofar as they are themselves unconscious, repeat this pattern, pushing their child with pride and joy, often much too fast, towards growth and maturity, and then, at the least sign of an independence that threatens their ascendancy, pulling him back into an infantile dependence.

Wotan proceeds to do just this. He has set the stage for the meeting of Siegmund with Sieglinda and has left the great sword Nothung in the tree in Hunding's dwelling. His son, Siegmund, meeting his sister-anima, finds at the same time his manhood, his sword (as Aragorn finds Arwen and is given his sword). The free man in Siegmund defies the laws of the gods and men in the service of his true love, and the evil Hunding will inevitably go down before the magic weapon. Wotan is pleased and proud of his son until Fricka, his hidebound conventional wife-anima, who will make life exceedingly uncomfortable for him if he condones any kind of rebellion against the time-honored laws of the gods, absolutely forbids him to allow Siegmund to win the fight. (What would the neighbors say?) Weakly he gives in and sends for his warrior daughter Brunhilde, whose mother is the Earth goddess Erda, and tells her to see to it that Hunding shall be victorious. Says Wotan, "Boldly I brought him up to flaunt the laws of the gods. Why did I want to break myself in this way? How easily Fricka found out the fraud. She saw right through me, all to my shame. I must yield my will to her purpose." Brunhilde is horrified at all this, and for the first time in her life she dares to disobey her father. She will carry out what she knows to be his real desire and defy his conventional orders.

Brunhilde's rebellion is a symbol of the crucial turning point in the psyche of every woman. It is the moment when she first stands by her own feeling, defying the father, the external authority by which she has lived. Brunhilde stands also for the true feeling of the father himself, which is why he is so excessively furious with her. She does not succeed in saving Siegmund, for Wotan himself, like so many human fathers, shatters with his spear the sword he himself had given to his son, but she does save Sieglinda and her unborn son before Wotan can stop her. Wotan's rejected feeling side fails to save his first attempt to create a free man, but she nevertheless makes possible a second chance in the future. She must now pay the price.

Brunhilde was the daughter of Wotan and Erda the Earth Mother, but she, like Siegfried, had evidently been taken from her mother and brought up entirely by her father. Her dealings with men consisted solely in collecting dead warriors from the battlefield and bringing them to Valhalla for the greater glory of her father Wotan. So a woman whose animus remains identified with an immensely powerful father image will have no use for a living man, and will unconsciously turn all her relationships with men into a sterile repetition of her tie to her father. She is indeed like a Valkyrie, bringing dead heroes to Valhalla, her free creativity stifled, and she gives out a feeling of not living quite on this earth. So also the father who binds his daughter to him with unconscious chains is using his potential creative feeling to protect himself from reality, and continually attempts to bolster up his prestige through obeying his "Fricka" anima. Brunhilde, however, rebels. She will not betray her own truth. In disobeying she is true not only to herself but to her father. How it recurs, this theme! Disobedience to authority, *at the right moment,* is the essential of any and every breakthrough of new awareness—disobedience with a condition, however. It is senseless and meaningless rebellion if it is not inspired by a real devotion to a conscious value and if there is not complete willingness at the same time to suffer the consequences, whatever they may be. Brunhilde knew that her disobedience would probably be punished by death. Wotan instead condemned her to her long sleep and to an awakening which would deprive her of her divinity.

Dr. Marie-Louise von Franz has said that there are women who are "asleep" and who often remain so for many years. As in the story of the Sleeping Beauty, nothing can awaken them except the seemingly fortuitous arrival of the "Prince." She points out that this sleep of woman, both collectively and individually, is caused by a devaluation of the feminine principle. For instance, a woman whose mother's animus has dominated her childhood may have grown up in the belief that she is quite worthless—that her personality has no meaning, and she simply stays out of life, goes to sleep. If she is wholly identified with her father's anima, the same sense of nonexistence as an individual holds sway. Collectively it is the same; the rejection of the feminine values—the attitude that women are inferior creatures, that they are in some way the source of all evil, from the serpent and Eve onwards—has been a dominant feature of our culture for centuries, and the central theme of this myth is the sterility and near-disaster that this rejection brings in the long run, the rejection of Eros that forges the ring of power and from which the world can be saved only by woman redeemed and conscious.

In this context we see clearly how significant it is that both Siegfried and Brunhilde have been nurtured by men, without mothers. Erda is certainly around, but she only rises up sleepily out of the earth from time to time and keeps asking Wotan to stop pestering her! The Earth Mother herself is sleeping. It is surely a man's world. The Germany of Hitler was the violent eruption into society of the absolute supremacy of the masculine; small wonder that the Nazis gave precedence to this myth over Christianity.

Brunhilde's disobedience, her stand for real feeling, is the seed of the re-emergence of the feminine—but, like all such seeds, it takes a long time to ripen. The new attitude rises for a moment in us and asserts itself in some act of rebellion, perhaps, but as yet it is too weak to live in the conscious world. The authorities that dominate this world push it down again, and it must sleep and wait. We may remember such a moment when we stood by our feelings in the teeth of all the generally accepted laws of our world but were not strong enough to maintain the barely glimpsed freedom. Now the woman lies sleeping, but not dead, and she is surrounded by fire. Only one who will fearlessly experience the fires of his own emotional nature can reach and wake her. A man's dormant capacity for conscious relationship is awakened only when he has passed through this fire.

The third part of the drama is the story of Siegfried's coming to manhood in the cave of the dwarf smith, Mime. Sieglinda having died when he was born, the boy had grown up in ignorance that such a thing as a mother existed—and his presumed father, Mime, certainly provided him with no heroic image. In such a situation he learned nothing of tenderness and love except from watching the birds and beasts, and it is interesting at this point to note the difference between Siegfried's education and Parsifal's in the Grail legend, especially as Wagner wrote *Parsifal* as a sequel to the Ring cycle. The quest of the Grail was to him the symbol of the new birth from the sacrifice of Brunhilde and Siegfried. Parsifal, in contrast to Siegfried, grew up without a father, alone in the woods with his adoring mother, and his need as a youth was to break away from his mother's apron strings, from too much femininity. He was too shy, too naïve in his feelings, too much afraid of offending. He failed to ask the right question on first coming to the Grail castle because he had been told that it was not polite to ask questions. Siegfried, on the other hand, could most certainly never be accused of a surfeit of courtesy. He is brash and boastful, and, contemptible as Mime is, one is left feeling irritated at Siefried's constant and overbearing rudeness. His need is to find the meaning of kindness and forbearance. He had never even met a woman. So it appears that the Siegfried type of hero, who has grown up unloved and must seek for all the unknown values of the heart, remains at the mercy of the unconscious, in spite of all his courage, in spite of Brunhilde even, falling blindly into Eros traps until the light breaks through at the moment of his death.

Siegfried, having reforged his father's sword, is goaded by Mime's clever insinuations into a determination to find out what fear is, and he storms off, shouting some more boasts, to find the dragon. Here is no chivalrous knight, spending a night in lonely vigil, before taking up his dragon-slaying task as a grown man; no simple primitive going through the pains of initiation to manhood in his tribe; and assuredly no Frodo choosing at the entry to the second half of life the necessity of his burden, in great fear but with complete acceptance—going out not to kill the dragon but to walk straight into its jaws in order to defeat it from within. Siegfried is, rather, the young adolescent male, aggressive, self-confident, bent only on getting—however idealistic his aims—what *he* wants, insensitive at first to anything else.

Jung in his autobiography tells the dream that came to him at the great turning point, after his parting from Freud, when he first began to confront the unconscious. He and a little primitive man together shot and killed Siegfried, who was driving at great speed a chariot made of the bones of the dead. The dreamer had an unbearable feeling of guilt and sorrow at what he had done, and when he awoke there was a sense of great urgency, so great that he knew he must understand this dream or kill *himself.* Then he saw that Siegfried stood for the German determination to heroically impose their will, to have their own way, and that he had been secretly identified with that attitude himself. Hence his grief in the dream over the death of the heroic idealism of the ego and its demand to conquer, which can be a thing of great beauty. But Siegfried was driving a chariot made of dead bones. His time was over. If Jung had in fact gone down into those deep places of the unconscious with the old Siegfried attitude of bending everything to his will, he would indeed have been lost; hence the terrible urgency.

Only a hero without fear is able to kill Fafnir. Innocence alone is wholly free from fear, whether it be the unconscious innocence of childhood or the final innocence of the Self, and in face of it, all conflict is done away. "The lion shall lie down with the lamb and a little child shall lead them." Siegfried is still in a state of innocence because although he is already a young man he has not yet experienced the split in his nature. Impulse and act are still one thing, everything is external and just what it seems; there are no shadows, no questions. Life is a simple, "I want, and I don't want." Such a man has an enormous strength— of a kind—for none of his energy is drained off into doubts and questionings. He does not kill the dragon for the sake of riches and power, nor for the sake of some ideal, nor because he is in danger. He simply kills the dragon because it is there in his way.

There are stirrings, however, in Siegfried. He has heard of this mysterious thing called fear and he is determined to find it. It is his first "quest"—and rightly, for without the experience of fear there is no fall and no redemption. Then just before he meets the dragon comes a moment of quiet (the first time he stops rushing about and roaring, it seems!). He dreams of his mother and father, and on awakening listens to a bird singing and is carried out of himself by a longing to understand what the bird is saying—that is, he has recognized that there is a language other than his own. He kills the dragon and he drinks the drop of blood, and with it the poison enters his being and his ears are opened to this new language. Siegfried experiences the Fall; he enters the split, and conscious experience begins, the knowledge of good and evil. In every myth and legend, in every human life, it is the same. The poison must enter into us, we must emerge from the infantile paradise, before we can ever set foot on the way to that which Blake calls "Fourfold Vision." We must drink a little of that which is poison to the conscious ego, but not too much, for if we drink too much we *become* the dragon, are swallowed by the unconscious.

The bird, the voice from within, now speaks to Siegfried, and in the manner of our dreams it both warns him of his danger and points the way to his next task. The poison of the archetypal dragon has entered his blood stream, and its immediate effect is to protect him against the threatened poisoning of his personal life by Mime. (It is the same principle as that of inoculation in medicine.) Innocently he would have fallen into the trap without the warning of the bird, but his innocence is broken. He destroys his enemy, defeats Mime, the personal shadow, and then discovers that he is lonely. It is this discovery of loneliness that sends a man off in search of his other side, his feminine soul; he has half-consciously recognized the need for relationship. So Siegfried goes to seek the fire through which he must pass to find both fear and love.

It is at this point, wearing the ring from the dragon's hoard, albeit quite unconscious of its power, that he meets Wotan, disguised as the Wanderer, and breaks the god's spear. The fight with the shadow always leads to this; the old ruling principle of consciousness that opposes the new way is challenged and its authority broken. From this moment it is clear that the downfall of the gods has begun. What remains in doubt is the manner of it and the succession. It is the same thing as in *The Lord of the Rings*. The time of the elves and wizards, of gods and demons must end, now that the ring is abroad in the world. Will it be succeeded by total destruction through the ego's use of power, or by the sacrifice of this power and the birth of the Self as ruler in the psyche of man?

There is a major difference in the symbolism of power in the two stories. As soon as he had forged the ring, Alberich used it to compel his slaves to amass a huge hoard of gold for him, and he says explicitly that he will come to world domination by exploiting men's greed for riches. Fafnir sat guarding his hoard, which was of greater importance to him than the ring he did not understand. In Wagner's time came the tremendous rise of power through money; huge personal fortunes were amassed, and the capitalists ruled from behind the scenes; gold was discovered in America and Australia, diamonds in South Africa, and thousands were seized with the fever to get rich quickly, sacrificing every other value to this passion.

We find an entirely different feeling in the twentieth-century story; there is hardly a mention of material riches from beginning to end. Our danger today is quite other and far greater. Power is sought and wielded for its own sake, often heavily disguised under the mask of selfless devotion to the public good. The fanatic of Communist or Nazi persuasion will suffer poverty and hardship, will undergo extreme ascetic discipline and will sacrifice personal desire and feeling, believing sincerely that he does all this for the good of humanity—and so the ring is delivered up to the Sauron in the unconscious whose rule means the ultimate destruction of love, of the free spirit of man, and of humanity itself. The fanatic is an extreme, but the belief in the use of power to compel the public good threatens us all, and the corruption spreads subtly into our social and political and, more dangerously still, into our religious attitudes. There was a paragraph in a religious paper recently that openly stated that people must be instructed in how to "use power" for good ends. The greed of gold is a harmless thing in comparison with this. The anti-Christ is precisely that which practices the Christian virtues for an end that leads to the power in *this* world, which Christ refused, and so to the rejection of the Kingdom of Heaven which is within.

As Jung points out, it is not surprising that the "angels" of today, the collective visions, are rings, circles—the flying saucers coming from outer space, from the remote depths of the psyche with a message either of total destruction, or if we turn inwards, of the vision of the Self, the totality. The choice lies with each single man; it is before us in every small choice of every day. Will we have power or love, totalitarianism or the totality?

Siegfried, then, was the man free from all subservience to the gods of his time. He never gave a thought to the hoard of gold—left it for any to take who would, and proceeded to break Wotan's spear by the power of the ring without knowing what he was doing. So unconsciously do the crude rebellions of youth shatter the old, and open the way to a new birth. We may be thankful that this, at least, is happening on a colossal scale today, but after the rebellion must come the hard work, the discipline and the suffering, or the rebellion becomes a mere swing from one opposite to the other, and the "dark lord" gathers the power to himself. Will we find the "Frodo" within to carry the ring to the fire?

To return to the myth, Siegfried, having shattered authority, passes through the emotional storms of youth, no longer innocent. He experiences, it may be imagined, his own passionate nature, and having shirked nothing he comes to the opportunity of love. At this point we may remember the barrier of fire through which Dante had to pass to reach Beatrice in the Earthly Paradise. It is the same symbol on an entirely different level of consciousness, and this is an example of how in our dreams the same symbols appear again and again, and we are apt to cry out, "I dreamed all that a year ago. Have I moved at all?" Beatrice, the meaning of love, must be discovered and rediscovered, on the spiral way, and at each major transformation of attitude a man must suffer the ordeal by fire. Dante passed through it to the final awareness which could lead him into the circles of Paradise to the "Love which moves the sun and the other stars" (*Paradiso*). Siegfried is the very young man who braves the emotional fires to find his first glimpse of responsible feeling.

This, however, is no story of the Prince who wakes his Sleeping Beauty and they live happily ever after; on the contrary, it is the beginning of Siegfried's experience of manhood, of Brunhilde's experience of mortality. Hitherto Siegfried has been a boy; now through the awakening of his first love comes the glimpse afar off of the beauty of the end, the final unity, and with the possession of the ring comes the beginning of responsibility. One night he spends with Brunhilde, and then he leaves her to prove himself as a man, giving her the ring to keep as a pledge of his love. This gift is the certain proof that Siegfried values love, undifferentiated though it still is for him, above power. The weakness and sin into which he now falls are not therefore a basic betrayal, they are a failure to grow *through* the personal romantic love into that other love that includes and transcends it. The gift of the ring to his personal love shows indeed his freedom from the power drive, but it also symbolizes his unconscious identification of his beloved with the totality, and his failure to take up the real responsibility of consciousness. This is the experience through which all young men of generous heart must pass when they fall in love. Then come the years of learning how to withdraw the projection without rejecting their love. And most, like Siegfried, must regress before the vital breakthrough to consciousness can be made. It comes to Siegfried only at the moment of his death.

In Brunhilde, too, the same pattern is clear. Warned by her sister that if she does not part from the ring it will bring disaster on gods and men, she will hear nothing. The ring is Siegfried's pledge of love and nothing else matters. Her personal love is the *whole* to her—no other value can possibly transcend it, and to women this is a more frequent danger than to men. Nevertheless, until a man or a woman has passed through this overwhelming experience of personal love in some form or other, he or she does not even set foot on the way to individuation. Nothing can be sacrificed—that is, transformed, made holy, purged of personal demand—unless it has first been fully possessed.

Like most of us then, Siegfried and Brunhilde proceed to learn the hard way. Siegfried has never confronted the shadow more than half-consciously. He has simply swept it out of the way imperiously with his all-conquering sword, with his personal will, brushing aside everything he does not understand. He killed Mime and the dragon, and broke Wotan's spear, but without a moment's reflection. He comes now to his meeting with Hagen in the castle by the Rhine and fails to recognize this new enemy, who traps him exactly the same way as Mime had tried to trap him—with a doctored drink. As an innocent boy he heard the warning of the bird in his heart. This time he no longer hears. He drinks the potion, forgets the love of his heart, and is gripped by a sensual passion for the first woman in sight. Not only that, but he proceeds to betray his true love by an impersonation of Gunther, trying to force Brunhilde, too, into a lesser love. In this he does not succeed, but, instead, her love turns for a disastrous moment into hatred for Siegfried himself. She reveals his weak spot to Hagen, and so, indirectly, is responsible for his death. It is the course of many a relationship, falling from the high promise of the first vision. As the beauty of the projection fades it is called "nothing but" and so betrayed. It is not consciously sacrificed

31

so that its reality may be reborn through the hard work of learning separateness and objective love.

Gunther and Gutrune are good, simple people. They agree to the fulfillment of their desires which Siegfried plans for them. How could such a great hero be wrong? But they are uneasy nevertheless. So is the truth of the simple humanity within us betrayed when the inner vision of beauty is pushed down into the unconscious by the wiles of the shadow unrecognized.

Siegfried falls lower yet. On the banks of the river the Rhine maidens rise up and plead for the ring, which Siegfried has forcibly taken back from Brunhilde. He refuses, and then indulges in fantasies about possessing one of these beautiful women, "if only he were not true to Gutrune." The maidens then threaten him with the consequences of keeping the ring for his personal use—and he at once regresses to his childish boastings about how fearless he is. We have a feeling he has hit bottom, and it is indeed so. At the request of Hagen, of the shadow himself, as so often, he begins at last to *reflect*, and his memory returns. He remembers the birds and speaks his first words of humility: "Since I heard women singing I have quite forgotten the birds." Most of us hear the birds singing in our youth, and most of us allow the loud songs of our emotional involvements to *replace* the sound of the birds. Only when we hear again the still, small voice do all the songs of the world become a great harmony. To Siegfried this moment comes when Hagen stabs him in the back. As so often, the shadow is the final instrument of full awakening (remember Gollum and Frodo). He has paid for all with his life, but he is awake, conscious at last of *meaning*. Brunhilde, aroused from sleep *within* him this time, is his forever as he dies. Hagen is powerless to take the ring, and it remains for Brunhilde to return it to the unconscious.

The fall of the gods is an inevitable outcome of the story of the ring. As in Tolkien's story, one way or another the old order is doomed. The manner of the fall is the vital theme, as we said earlier. The ring in the hands of the collective shadow would have utterly destroyed the old gods, but through Brunhilde's conscious sacrifice they are burned in a fierce purging fire, and there is a hope of rebirth. Nevertheless there is something unsatisfying about Brunhilde's leap into the fire with Grane, the horse. Brunhilde is an image of immature womanhood, however noble her sacrifice. She was incapable of consent to a life of loneliness, to the bearing of Siegfried's child without either projected gods or personal love to help her carry the burden, and so the most she could do was to return the ring to the water maidens in the unconscious to be their plaything until the next theft and the next forging.

For Wagner as an individual artist, the cycle of the ring gave birth to his vision of the Quest of the Grail in which transformation and redemption are achieved; but for the German psyche collectively the Siegfried myth has, hitherto, been all too often the final word. Nietsche was furious with Wagner for writing *Parsifal,* for "selling out" on the superman, so to speak, and replacing the dead gods with a living symbol of Christ, of the Self. In common with great numbers of his countrymen, Nietsche ended by identifying his ego disastrously with the superman. Thus the whole story has been repeated again and again. Siegfried, the courageous and idealistic thing in the German character, rises and slays the dragon of sloth (think of the miraculous power of recovery after each defeat in Germany), takes the ring to himself, but remains so unconscious, so childish in the feeling area, that he is betrayed by the Alberich shadow over and over again into the dream of ruling the world, and so to such horrors as the Nazi creed. From this dream the "master race" can be saved only by defeat, which brings the Brunhilde, the feeling value in the unconscious, back to awareness. But the most she can do is to return the ring to the water before dying with her Siegfried.

The story of Frodo is on another level. It is not only myth; it tells of the living of the myth by conscious human beings. It speaks to us of the possibility of final success through *individuation,* the coming to consciousness of the values of spirit and flesh, of intellect and heart, and the consummation of the *hierosgamos* here on earth.

It might be said that in Tolkien's story there are very few women who play more than a brief part in the action. Yet in contrast to the Siegfried myth there is never any sense at all of a devaluation or repression of the feminine. On the contrary, feminine values are the very ground of the whole story. The hobbits themselves are a people rooted in the simplicities of feeling, and it is because they are so well related to the earth, to the heart, that they are capable of undertaking the great journey, of awakening to the high purpose of the masculine principle seeking its goal without the near-certainty of falling victim to the power drive of the one-sidedly male psyche. The flame of the spirit burns bright and clear in this book, piercing through all the dark shadows to its goal, because it is fed and nourished by the warmth of the heart.

The women are in the background, but are nonetheless vital to the quest. When the feminine usurps the place of the head, of the leader in the outer world, says the *I Ching*, then there is war between the two principles, and both spirit and heart are damaged. But when she nourishes the spirit from within, there is wholeness. Galadriel and Shelob, Arwen and Eowyn, little Rosie waiting for her Sam—all are vital to the story. Galadriel, the anima who is the inner guide of man, alone can give Frodo the phial of light that saves him when he must meet the overwhelming onslaught of the devouring feminine, Shelob. Arwen, the queen, is the symbol of the numinous anima in man who yet submits to mortality, so that her lover becomes rooted in true relatedness on this earth. Eowyn, the cold "Shield-maiden," has been asleep, as Brunhilde was asleep, and is awakened by Aragorn, who nevertheless must leave her. Unlike Siegfried, he does not betray Eowyn, he is simply true to himself in leaving her, and she goes to her courageous sacrifice on battlefield just as Brunhilde went knowingly into the fire. The king of the Ringwraiths is destroyed by her, and the danger of Gondor's defeat is averted, just as the danger from the ring was averted by Brunhilde's action. She courts death, but unlike Brunhilde she has not deliberately killed herself, and she survives and goes on to her complete *human* awakening to love, and her marriage with Faramir follows in the newly redeemed kingdom of Gondor.

Brunhilde, too, has a second awakening, but it cannot live as yet in this world. Here is the basic difference in the two stories. Brunhilde, the feminine principle in the myth, never in fact finds her place in the ground of being. It is she at the last who is playing the active role. The man, the spirit, has refused to part with the ring and so has died by treachery. The woman completes his task and *deliberately* enters the fire, taking Grane, their horse, symbol of man's basic libido, with her. We are left with the feeling that the whole cycle has ended in destruction—that everything has taken place in the unconscious. Nothing has won through to incarnation. It has been a tremendous and magnificent attempt, and no such attempt can be called a failure, because in fact the ring was saved from those who would use it to destroy consciousness; but on the other hand it is only a negative success. Siegfried, the man, has gone under, and his anima must inevitably go with him. Brunhilde's dramatic immolation of herself is yet another image of the devaluation of the feminine principle. Hindu women were burned on their husband's funeral pyre because they were of value only as appendages of men and had no existence in their own right. As long as this attitude remains there can be no hierosgamos, no conscious union of male and female, no final end to the rule of ego power.

Siegfried and Brunhilde are great symbols of the generous enthusiasms of youth; the tragedy lies in their inability to grow to maturity. Frodo's "coming of age" is his thirty-third birthday—and on this day his awakening to his conscious quest begins. Jung wrote of the desperate need of Western man for this taking up of the conscious search for wholeness at the midpoint of life. At this time, if we are not to follow Siegfried into his decline, when his innocence became childish gullibility and the voice of the bird was no longer heard in his heart, we must "kill" Siegfried, the golden hero of youth, as Jung killed him in his dream, and find Frodo, the simple devotion and dogged courage that will take up and carry through the *inner* journey. To him we must deliver up the ring of power that he may carry it through extreme danger and suffering to the fire which alone can destroy it utterly, or rather, since nothing can be finally destroyed, transform it into the circle of human wholeness here on this earth. All the final chapters of the book are concerned with this newly born harmony in ordinary human life. Frodo has no superficially heroic dimensions. He simply goes on from one day to the next, through despair and beyond it, and as he goes, Sam sees a kind of light growing within his master. At the edge of doom, he achieves no great sacrificial gesture; on the contrary, Gollum, his personal shadow, to whom he has shown constant compassion, is the agent of his final success. We could not imagine him deliberately martyring himself. Only his *ring finger* is burnt with the ring in the fire, a symbol, surely, of the final breaking of every *unconscious* tie or bond, of his coming to the "perfect liberty" which is love. At the end of *The Twilight of the Gods* there is indeed a hint of the same solution, for only one person remains alive—Gutrune, the ordinary human woman who has been throughout a simple-hearted victim of the doings of hero, heroine, and villains. She fades into the background before the climax and is easy to forget, but she is there, a human being who can begin again.

In Tolkien's story the very last image of all is of Sam by his fireside with his wife and child, and it is borne in upon us that the whole tremendous story of light and darkness, of great deeds and betrayals, of kings and wizards and demons has been played out to establish one value, one meaning beyond all others—the simple human wholeness of a true man, a true woman, and their child.

REFLECTIONS ON SHAKESPEARE

INTRODUCTION

In Stratford, Ontario in 1976 I heard and saw three stories told. The storytellers were Shakespeare himself, the directors, the actors and actresses, and the potential teller of stories in myself and in each and all of the huge audience. The plays were *The Merchant of Venice, Antony and Cleopatra,* and *The Tempest.*

Any story, when touched by the magic of the authentic storyteller, has in some degree a transforming power, and as we respond to such a tale we are for a moment lifted out of our preoccupation with small goals and changed. A real story need hold no surprises; the better it is known, the more profoundly it may be enjoyed. Anyone who has told their favorite stories to imaginative children knows this; there must be no deviation in the telling, and the wonder and delight of the child increase with each repetition; the suspense, the sudden denouements lose none of their power. We know how vitally important the story-tellers and minstrels were to all primitive cultures, preserving for each generation the essential links to the ancestors and to the myths that sustain all men. But with the coming of the written word to the child, as to the primitive, delight in the old stories is dimmed by the growing demand for the expansion of knowledge, which is, of course, essential to the growth of consciousness. If, however, this expansion is allowed to destroy the life of Story then the new knowledge itself is a dead thing. Fortunately there are, and always have been, the poets among men by whom the wonder of Story is kept alive.

As so often, one word — "story" — is used to express two widely differing things. A narrative of happenings which never touches the inner springs of poetry and meaning, and a transforming tale of the kind we are discussing here are both called *stories.* We are in the same difficulty with the word *imagination.* It may describe something untrue ("He only imagined it," we say), but it also means the creative image-making through which we grow into wholeness. In the second sense of both words, stories spring from life-giving imagination; they are the links between outer facts and myth.

It is not by chance that the greatest of the poets: Homer, Dante, Shakespeare—and, to extend the list, Aeschylus, Milton, Blake, Virgil, Molière, and the unknown poets of the Bible—all tell stories of such immense scope, reaching from the outer events of human lives down into the depths of the unconscious psyche. They invoke gods and demons while at the same time leaving us with unforgettable images of the simplest things—the "wine-dark sea" of Homer, the "dark wood" of Dante, the "bank where the wild thyme grows" of Shakespeare—to quote at random from the innumerable tiny pictures left to us by these three masters. The reason we never forget them is that they evoke in us that other dimension whereby they cease to be fact alone and become *symbol,* and so a part of Story. The wine-dark sea carries the black ship of Odysseus on his inner as well as his outer journey; the dark wood of Dante is an experience known to every human being who has lost all sense of meaning in his life; and Titania's magic influence is alive in all men, as she sleeps on that bank where thyme grows and the snake sheds its skin.

To those storytellers who have written drama we owe a particular debt, for our imagination is given an enormous stimulus by the opportunity to see their stories brought to life through the imaginations of interpreters who re-enact them on the stage. Great theater frees us from the ego in those hours of looking and listening; but as we emerge into common concerns of every day, we put on again the blinkers of the prosaic, and the experience may easily sink into the realm of forgotten things. As I drove home from Stratford I was musing about this, and it occurred to me that if we could make the effort after each performance to retell the story evoked by the great poet with our own associations and perceptions of meaning, so that it became imaginatively linked to our personal life stories, perhaps then we might remember more often how the most ordinary of our daily concerns could be felt as a part of a living tale instead of as meaningless repetitions. I often think of Sam in *The Lord of the Rings,* when he suddenly saw himself and Frodo as part of a great story, which had begun in the distant past and would go on when their part in it should be over.

The way back to the wonder of the child as he or she listens to a story becomes possible for many people in our time through the discovery of the stories that come to us in our dreams, opening a door into the symbolic life. Even when the images seem banal, we feel an enhanced life if we allow them to transform the narrative of our lives into a Story, so that we begin to listen and observe objectively instead of being identified with each happening. So, before the impact of the plays I saw at Stratford fades, I want to make an attempt, as though confronted with a dream, to put into words the response of the "storyteller" in myself.

Shakespeare's plays are often heard superficially, and the deeper story is lost in the easy sensations evoked by situations of dramatic suspense and romance. Shakespeare could most surely delight an unthinking audience with these things, but never from the beginning was this the whole of any play. As Harold C. Goddard repeatedly points out, underneath the entertainment of the plays lies the story told by Shakespeare the poet, and it is heard by those who are awake to it in increasing depth as they grow older, and as repetition opens door after door of perception. The archetype of the Storyteller may then come to life in each hearer so that he or she somehow has a feeling of *creating with* the poet in a small way, through the fire of his or her response.

Large quantities of drama and fiction are produced to meet the human need for entertainment, and Shakespeare drew on many transient plays or tales, as well as on historical records. There are a variety of stories in *The Merchant of Venice,* for instance—the bond, the caskets, the elopement of Jessica—and these have been traced to different sources, most of them without interest except as material for Shakespeare's genius. Like many great artists he surely felt no qualms of conscience at all about his borrowings. He would have agreed with Molière who, when accused of plagiarism, replied, *"Je prends mon bien ou je le trouve"*—literally, "I take my 'good' wherever I find it." In other words, the other man's story *belongs* to him because he has made it his own by linking it to the great mystery of his own inner story.

At this point I want to pay tribute to Goddard and his book, *The Meaning of Shakespeare.* I had read and seen Shakespeare plays in my childhood and youth, and had been inspired by all the obvious things and certainly moved by the poetry. Conscious insights, however, can actually be inhibited by a familiarity acquired in youth, and the reading of Goddard's book some years ago opened my mind to new and rich depths in the plays. It will be obvious in my attempt to retell for myself the stories contained in these plays how much I owe to his retelling of them. Reading his book we realize the gulf between intellectual analysis of a story and penetration by the reader to its meaning for him or her personally—which is in fact the retelling of the story itself.

Shakespeare's plays are fundamentally concerned with the nature of power and of love and with their realization in the lives of individuals. Indeed, for those who seek wholeness, the split between these two instinctual drives is the essential material of the journey into consciousness. Where there is no real love, the power drive inevitably takes over the ego and fills the vacuum; where there is no individual responsibility toward the powers that are given to each of us in our degree, the travesty of love which is personal greed is in control. This is particularly clear, as we shall see, in *Antony and Cleopatra.* The poetry of Shakespeare turns us again and again toward the only final resolution of the split—not the overcoming of power by love, but their final unity in which love is power and power is love.

The Merchant of Venice

This play tells a story of hatred, of dark vengeance and cruelty, and of the defeat of these things on the surface by a woman of great intelligence—one of Shakespeare's line of enchanting heroines who disguise themselves as men on their way to the fruition of their womanhood. There is, however, a profound difference between the fascination of Portia and the quality of such women as Rosalind or Viola. The latter two are at one with themselves; but in Portia Shakespeare seems to have leapt the centuries, showing us a woman in the grip of the conflict with which we are today so very familiar. We shall see how Portia swings between destructive possession by a potentially creative animus and a true feminine wisdom through which her masculine spirit speaks at rare intervals in the power of love.

At the outset of the play, if we are able to understand it in depth, we need to be aware of the prevailing atmosphere of boredom, stressed by Goddard—a state of mind that weighs heavily on the principal characters other than Shylock. In the opening speech of the play Antonio, the merchant, states it:

> In sooth, I know not why I am so sad:
> It wearies me; you say it wearies you;
> But how I caught it, found it, or came by it,
> What stuff 'tis made of, whereof it is born,
> I am to learn;
> And such a want-wit sadness makes of me
> That I have much ado to know myself.
> (I.1)[1]

That is the point: Antonio is rich, cultivated, kindhearted, respected, even loved, but he does not know himself, and therefore he is bored, as all men are bored who possess the good things that money can buy but have no awareness of the shadow in themselves. He himself puts it the other way round and says that his boredom prevents his self-knowledge, thus excusing himself, in a way we know only too well, from the effort to know himself, which is the one cure for boredom. His friends suggest external causes for his sadness—anxiety for his ships at sea, love of a lady—but these he denies at once, clinging to the "sad part" he feels condemned by fate to play in the world. If he did but know it, his boredom is due precisely to the fact that he is *not* "in love," and, we feel, probably never has been; nor for that matter is he "in fear," being too sure of his worldly wealth. Even his devotion to Bassanio, while it is the best thing about him, has also become through blindness a channel for vicarious living.

Boredom is invariably the result of being cut off from the springs of life in the unconscious. A spontaneous person who lives close to nature is never bored and never boring, but those who have reached a state where they *could* begin to know themselves and are evading it will inevitably feel the weight of boredom, in spite of all their attempts to escape it through the pursuit of knowledge, through lust of all kinds, through good works, or through wit that has no humor in it.

Antonio's boredom has opened the play. Now at the beginning of act I, scene 2, Portia speaks.

> By my troth, Nerissa, my little body is aweary of this great world.

And Nerissa observes:

> They are as sick that surfeit with too much, as they that starve with nothing.

Portia, too, is bored, and although her animus can, as is usual, dispense abstract wisdom most competently and delude her into thinking she understands herself, she is really as blind to her shadow as is Antonio.

> If to do were as easy as to know what were good to do,
> chapels had been churches, and poor men's cottages princes'
> palaces. It is a good divine that follows his own instructions: I
> can easier teach twenty what were good to be done, than be
> one of the twenty to follow mine own teaching.
> (I.2)

Excellent and perceptive talk, but she does not take seriously its application to her own *specific* behavior. This is a sure sign of the domination of secondhand opinions in a woman. After her moralizing speech, Portia proceeds to tell us of her dead father's will, whereby she is forbidden to make her own choice of a husband. She is to marry only the man who chooses rightly between three caskets—the gold, the silver, and the lead. "So is the will of a living daughter curbed by the will of a dead father" (I.2). By our standards she is spiritless indeed to be bound by this, to allow the dead hand of authority to dictate the love of her heart. But Nerissa gives us a clear pointer to the symbolic nature of the caskets, causing us to realize that a tradition that is dead in its outer form may yet leave a legacy of inner wisdom to guide our choices. There is no mention of Portia's mother, but Nerissa at the beginning of the play seems to be the voice of Portia's real femininity. It is interesting that when, later on, Portia comes more and more under the domination of the negative animus, Nerissa loses her individual savor, becoming a mere copy of her mistress, which, if we think of her as carrying Portia's potential feminine wisdom, is just what we should expect. Here at the outset Nerissa speaks wisely of Portia's father.

> The lottery that he hath devised in these three chests of gold,
> silver and lead—whereof who chooses his meaning chooses
> you—will, no doubt never be chosen by any rightly, but who
> you shall rightly love.
> (I.2)

The wisdom her father has left to her is "Do not give yourself to any man except one who is willing to 'give and hazard all he hath' (the motto on the lead casket)—never to one who is glittered by collective values ('who chooseth me shall gain what many men desire,' reads the gold casket), nor one who is fool enough to believe that he deserves success ('who chooseth me shall get as much as he deserves,' says the silver casket)" (II.7). Her old father knew that love is a giving and a hazarding of everything we are—not a fulfillment of ambition or a reward for virtue.

Portia at this point brushes aside Nerissa's grave reflection and treats us to a brilliant display of wit at the expense of her suitors, whom she finds boring and repellent. It is most entertaining, and we are apt to overlook the obvious fact that Portia, like Antonio, banishes her weariness of life by evading all attention to its true cause and projecting it onto others. In both Antonio and Portia, however, their repressed creative possibilities are pressing into consciousness. There is a hidden state of turmoil within that can lead to a breakthrough of new life. We expect in such a case some overwhelming experience, beginning outside and penetrating within, or beginning interiorly and coming to expression outwardly. Antonio is subjected to a terrible outer experience, and although he does not allow it to bring him to compassion and love, yet, as we shall see, the director and actor at Stratford indicated a hint of hope for him at the very end of the play. Portia, at the coming of Bassanio, is awakened by the birth of a real love in her, which leads to a revelation of her great potential inward beauty, and although she slips back into triviality and worse, her fundamental love for Bassanio remains as a promise for the future.

In the opening scenes, Portia's hidden destructiveness is revealed in her feminine sharp-tongued gossip, while Antonio, by a new action of unselfish kindness towards Bassanio, admirable in itself, awakens in us a suspicion about the dark side of this "good" man's character. Any woman who has begun to know her animus will recognize Portia's escape from herself, and a man whose anima is of a soft and maternal nature will know the situation into which Antonio falls.

The love between the young man Bassanio and Antonio, his older friend, is tender and true, and yet we at once realize Antonio's immaturity. His lack of awareness of his own darkness makes him blind to the flaws in Bassanio's character, for he offers all he has without conditions to the young man who has been borrowing money from him, spending it thoughtlessly, and coming back for more. Some people blindly accept Bassanio as a fine romantic hero, but what of his words in scene 1? He confesses his debts in noble accents and says:

> But my chief care
> Is to come fairly off from the great debts
> Wherein my time, something too prodigal,
> Hath left me gag'd. To you, Antonio,
> I owe the most, in money and in love.
> (I.1)

He then goes on to say that if Antonio will lend him three thousand ducats more he will hope to use the money to get enough to pay all his debts—a typical spendthrift's argument. Antonio says he doesn't care what it is for; Bassanio can have anything he wants—a typical doting parent's reply. Bassanio then divulges that his hope of repaying lies in marriage with a rich woman, and he needs money with which to woo her—no nonsense about hard work or thrift; all is to be put right with *her* money.

> In Belmont is a lady richly left,
> And she is fair. . . .
> . . .
> Her name is Portia. . . .
> . . .
> Nor is the wide world ignorant of her worth;
> For the four winds blow in from every coast
> Renowned suitors, and her sunny locks
> Hang on her temples like a golden fleece.
> (I.1)

No doubt he was sincere about her worth of character and her golden beauty, but the words "worth" and "golden" have a double meaning. Nevertheless, Bassanio is a young man capable of love and real generosity and the ability to "give and hazard all he hath," as he proves by his choice of the lead casket and by his response to Antonio's tragedy.

Antonio, not having the ready money, applies to Shylock, the rich Jew, for a loan until Antonio's ships come home, which he is certain will be before three months are gone. Shylock appears on the stage, and in contrast to the vibrating life in this miser of a despised race, the world-weary Antonio and his lightweight companions seem dim and gray. It is impossible to imagine that this man who is the "villain" of the piece, though he might be damned, could ever be bored. His vitality, his greatness, indeed, lie precisely in the fact that he is in love—in love with his money for its own sake, not for the pleasures that it buys or the ease it brings. Shakespeare's genius, if we hear the inner story of this play, makes us feel that the passionate love of anything for its own sake, however perverted and exclusive the object, and the bitter whole-hearted hatred that is its reverse side, are more life-giving and hold more promise of eventual redemption than any lukewarm undiscriminating kindness like Antonio's, of which the reverse side is a fastidious contempt.

At this meeting of Shylock and Antonio we are shown the clearest possible picture of two men meeting their projected shadows. Shylock meets in Antonio the unconscious and rejected goodness in himself and hates it; Antonio meets his unacknowledged avarice and ruthlessness personified in Shylock and treats it with withering contempt—a far more deadly thing than hatred. It is, I believe, because of this contempt that our sympathy for the Jew is awakened and remains with him to the end, even increasing as we see him more and more terrifyingly possessed by the demon of revenge. At Stratford there was a gesture that immensely enhanced the contrast between the qualities of the two men. Shylock put his hand on Antonio's arm for a moment and Antonio drew back with a movement of physical revulsion and disgust; it was a detail adding even greater power to the impact of Shylock's heart-rending speech later in the play.

> Hath not a Jew eyes? hath not a Jew hands, organs, dimen-
> sions, senses, affections, passions? fed with the same food,
> hurt with the same weapons, subject to the same diseases,
> healed by the same means, warmed and cooled by the same
> winter and summer as a Christian is?
> (III.1)

Hatred does not preclude respect, but contempt by its very nature robs its object of all dignity as a human being, and therefore is far more damaging to the soul of the one who feels it than hatred is. The "kinder" we are in our outward behavior, the more wary we need to be of that often very subtle kind of contempt that may be hidden in what may seem no more than a mild feeling of dislike or boredom. Antonio's gesture of physical repulsion toward another human being in this production shed a sudden brilliant light on the inner bankruptcy of this philanthropist.

Shylock's shadow side is his unrecognized potential generosity and kindness. His reiterated insistence on the moral justification of usury, of his right to high returns on his loans, together with his hatred of Antonio's practice of lending money without interest, gives away his inner uncertainty—even his envy of such a man. Goddard suggests that Shylock's offer to lend the three thousand ducats without interest is a genuine attempt to be generous and to offer friendship to Antonio. I do not think the text justifies this. I would rather say that it is one of those confused urges from the unconscious shadow which is immediately distorted by the ego's habitual attitude and used in such a way as to make it more destructive than the straightforward demand for high interest would have been. Although Shylock, knowing Antonio's resources, cannot at that point have had any real expectation of collecting the "pound of flesh" (and therefore calls his bargain a "merry bond"), it is plainly the expression of a murderous hatred in a fantasy of power over Antonio's life instead of over his money. Half-conscious fantasies are exceedingly dangerous and threaten all of us; if they are not recognized and confronted, they are more than likely to be realized literally, though we may of course easily refuse to be aware of the connection between the event and the fantasy.

Anything less "merry" than Shylock's bond could scarcely be imagined. A shadow quality half-recognized and then *used* by the ego is somehow doubly destructive; and this is equally true whether the shadow is positive or negative. For instance, a complacent admission of and apology for some dark thing in one's personality can often feed a man's sense of his own goodness and become a device for evading real responsibility for the shadow. So the "merry bond" is a confirmation and a deepening of Shylock's rejection of his own impulses toward generosity. The collection of the bond, however, remains a fantasy and is obviously so thought of by Shylock himself, until it is violently converted into a settled purpose in the outer world by Jessica's elopement with a Christian and her theft of her father's money and jewels, plus the fateful coincidence of Antonio's losses.

In act II we pass from the ego and shadow dramas of act I to the world of the anima and the animus. We watch the failure of Portia's two suitors who choose the gold and silver caskets respectively. They may symbolize for us the dangers to which the unconscious animus in women is always exposed. How easily indeed is he beguiled by following "what many men desire," the glittering opinions and causes that a woman often mistakes for the true gold. "All that glisters is not gold. . . Gilded tombs do worms infold" (II.7). Or, choosing the silver casket, he is forever concerned with his deserts, being by turns inflexibly "right" or hopelessly inadequate, swinging between inflation and deflation. "Am I superior, am I inferior?" Inside the silver casket is a picture of a fool's head.

In the case of a man, of course, all this applies to the nature of his anima, and reveals the dangers of being blind to the real values of relationship and love. These two types of men have no wish for a relationship with an individual woman—only with a collectively acceptable cipher—"what many men desire"; or else they suffer from the delusion that relationship is a matter of "rights."

Jessica, in this act, elopes with Lorenzo, and Shylock feels deserted and betrayed by his own flesh and blood. "My own flesh and blood to rebel!" he exclaims and repeats, "I say, my daughter is my flesh and my blood" (III.1). In other words, from this point on he is cut off from all the warmth and capacity for love which is indeed a man's psychic "flesh and blood." His daughter-anima has *rebelled* against his possessiveness and avarice and has allied herself with his shadow, with his potential tolerance and warmth of feeling (Lorenzo), and together they have disappeared into the unconscious and left his ego entirely cut off from his heart of "flesh and blood." Shakespeare's emphasis on this image here is surely deliberate. Are we not meant to remember it when Shylock demands the pound of flesh from Antonio's heart? His daughter, his symbolic "flesh and blood," has been stolen from him. He will seek to fill that awful vacuum by demanding the actual flesh and blood of the one on whom he projects his own responsibility for the loss. Thus do men and women try to compensate for their loss of soul by the demand for "just" compensation in the outer world. Whenever we have a burning sense of being cheated or being judged unfairly, a memory of Shylock's demand for flesh and blood could turn our attention inward to question what values in ourselves we have driven into the unconscious by a blind rejection, leaving a terrible emptiness in their place.

Jessica has, moreover, stolen money from her father and wounded him in his most vulnerable spot, for he loves money with passion as a woman is loved; she has also taken jewels and, in particular, one that he had especially loved because it held memories of his dead wife. There is a hint here of a true devotion still remembered and mourned, but now disastrously identified with the gold that glistens. So in act III with horror and compassion we see this man of potential greatness succumbing to an invasion from the unconscious in which all values of the heart are finally submerged. It is clear how wholly his love for his daughter and his real suffering for her loss have become identified with his possessions, but which of us can cast a stone after that terrible speech revealing what cruelty and contempt can do to a fellow man? "If a Jew wrong a Christian, what is his humility? Revenge. . . . The villainy you teach me I will execute" (III.1). Hume Cronyn in the Stratford production conveyed to us unforgettably this piercing tragedy of a man, whose capacity for love and devotion is very great, as he succumbs to possession by that very devotion in its most destructive form—the passion for revenge.

The evil of revenge is not lessened by the facts of extreme provocation, but Shakespeare does not allow his audience to escape their individual guilt in this matter. The compassion for Shylock, which all but the most insensitive must feel, leads surely, if we allow it to become fully conscious, to the recognition that each of us through his or her own unconscious shadow carries a responsibility for the darkness lived out by others. "The villainy you teach me I will execute." Contempt for the sins of others dies if we really hear these words, and we realize that to the exact extent that we do not confront and take responsibility for our own negative urges, we do in fact "teach" or shift on to others the burden of executing the villainies of which we are complacently unconscious. Shylock's cry, so often blindly laughed at, "My ducats and my daughter," is a shameful gloating joke spoken by Salarino in imitation of "the dog Jew." It is true that Shylock mourned them both equally, but he also said, "I would my daughter were dead at my foot. . . and the ducats in her coffin" (III.1). For a moment it seems that he is almost capable of realizing that where there is no love and compassion money is completely without value or meaning. But he cannot take the next step from this half-glimpsed truth. Jessica is left dead in the coffin, and his ducats, in the event, are also lost to him, because he has refused all warmth of feeling. So Shylock irrevocably chooses the golden casket, identifying the glittering thing with true gold, and is condemned to find within it the skull.

Goddard rightly condemns Jessica's treatment of her father, her theft of his money, though I feel he is too hard in his judgment of Jessica herself, who is going through a necessary adolescent rebellion. She is rescuing the core of her being from the dead hand of possessiveness and authority; she is saving her freedom to love, and although it would have certainly been a more creditable thing in her to have left empty-handed, yet, considering the atmosphere of greed for money in which she had grown up, it is hard to judge her act simply as a betrayal. It is, of course, no excuse for theft that society or the parents owe the younger generation a debt; such collective attitudes are always an escape. Yet

Jessica's act is surely understandable at this moment in her life. She will pay for it in due time.

While Jessica asserts her hatred of Shylock's miserly possessiveness and rejects him, a perceptive actress—as Domini Blythe this year at Stratford undoubtedly was—will surely affirm the one or two hints in the text of true sadness in her parting thought of her father: "I have a father, you a daughter, lost" (III.6). Both Jessica and her father have the chance through the personal loss to find love. We hear little more of Jessica; but Lorenzo, the man she loves, is seen at the end to be a poet—a lover of music—and it is hinted that together they will see beyond the outer shell of false gold to the inner content. Lorenzo, lying with her under the night sky, speaks:

> Look how the floor of heaven
> Is thick inlaid with patines of bright gold;
> There's not the smallest orb which thou behold'st
> But in his motion like an angel sings,
> Still quiring to the young-eyed cherubims.
> Such harmony is in immortal souls,
> But, whilst this muddy vesture of decay
> Doth grossly close it in, we cannot hear it.
> (V.1)

Act III tells of Bassanio's choice of the leaden casket, and with that choice comes the beginning of his transformation from a romantic, thoughtless boy into a man fully committed to love, to friendship, and to responsibility for the disastrous consequence of his former shallow spoilt-child attitude to life. For immediately after his choice and the awakening of love between Portia and himself comes the news of Antonio's losses and the forfeiture of his bond to Shylock. The Jew is demanding his pound of flesh in literal fact. The shock awakens Bassanio from his adolescent dreams and immediately he confesses to Portia his self-deceptions:

> Dear lady,
> Rating myself at nothing, you shall see
> How much I was a braggart. When I told you

My state was nothing, I should then have told you
That I was worse than nothing; for, indeed,
I have engaged myself to a dear friend,
Engaged my friend to his mere enemy
To feed my means.
 (III.2)

He goes at once to Venice to stand by his friend, leaving his newfound wife to live "as maid and widow" until his return. But Portia, we realize later, has immediately seen the flaw in the Jew's legal case. She has a dazzlingly quick mind (a hint of it was in her caricatures of the suitors at the beginning) and, as so many women do, she penetrates at once to the detail that destroys the logic of Shylock's case. The masculine mind, concerned passionately with principles—in this case, with the basic necessity of justice in the State—will often ignore the particular aspects of the actual situation in an affirmation of undoubted truth. The woman's animus, when operating in a manner disconnected from femininity, will do the same thing in an inferior and much more dangerous way, especially when the issue involves the ego's prestige; but when the woman's feminine feeling for the small and the particular is added to a true spirit of masculine clarity in her, then something can happen as it happened to Portia; she sees in the terms of the bond itself the way to a justice even more literal than Shylock's. Being Portia, with her love of the dramatic, she is not content to communicate her insight to the men concerned; she will go herself, disguised as a man of the law, to play the part of liberator. She is obviously about to enjoy herself immensely. She has been for a long time in a state of weary boredom, "surfeited with too much" and besieged by shallow fortune-hunters, and suddenly she is faced with a situation involving a man's life or death. She generously offers any amount of money to save Antonio, but it is already fairly certain that this time her money cannot buy immunity; and we feel she is somehow glad of it. It is a tremendously exciting challenge to her bored mind and her adventurous spirit. She, and so many women like her, because they are thus starved in mind and spirit, lose touch with the quiet satisfaction that may come to a woman whose insight transforms a situation without any dramatic performance by her ego. We may be thankful that Portia was not so mature or there would have been no play!

Portia pretends to Lorenzo that she is going away meekly to a monastery to pray, and then confides to Nerissa, with her usual sparkling wit, her plan to masquerade as a man.

> I'll hold thee any wager,
> When we are both accoutred like young men,
> I'll prove the prettier fellow of the two. . . .
>
> I have within my mind
> · A thousand raw tricks of those bragging Jacks
> Which I will practice.
> (III.4)

If we pause to think beyond the glitter, all this strikes a jarring note indeed against the background of her new and much-loved husband's terrible anxiety and the horror with which his friend is faced. From now on, the two levels of the play are closely interwoven—the exciting, dramatic entertainment and the fundamental drama of human suffering. In the trial scene we watch Portia herself swing from one level to the other, and we realize that she is capable of affirming not only the literal but the true justice that embraces mercy. Through her there might have come a reconciliation of the opposites through compassion. She might even have penetrated into the heart of the tortured Jew as well as revealing to the self-righteous, though courageous, Antonio a glimpse of his own darkness; but her vision is submerged again.

At the beginning of the trial the Duke makes an appeal to Shylock with dignity and courtesy. Shylock's answer to this is strangely moving, as we recognize within its violence a kind of dark greatness and dignity. It is as though he says, "You ask me to give up my rights in order to save your feelings in this matter; but I too have feelings every bit as strong as yours and as valid; I will stand by my feeling, no matter how cruel I may be thought."

> You'll ask me why I rather choose to have
> A weight of carrion flesh than to receive
> Three thousand ducats: I'll not answer that,
> But say, it is my humor. Is it answer'd?

> What if my house be troubled with a rat
> And I be pleased to give ten thousand ducats
> To have it baned? What, are you answer'd yet?
> Some men there are love not a gaping pig;
> Some that are mad if they behold a cat. . . .
> So can I give no reason, nor I will not,
> More than a lodged hate and a certain loathing
> I bear Antonio.
>   (IV.1)

I shall not easily forget Hume Cronyn as he spoke these lines. There is a kind of terrible courage and honesty in this that somehow shows up the dishonesty of feeling of the "good" man who has in fact treated the Jew over and over again as a rat to be spat upon, a pig to be shunned, a cat to be kicked and driven away, denying him all respect as an individual.

At this point Bassanio rises to his best, offering to die in place of Antonio. Antonio answers with the same essential world-weary attitude we heard in the first scene of the play.

> I am a tainted wether of the flock,
> Meetest for death; the weakest kind of fruit
> Drops earliest to the ground, and so let me:
> You cannot better be employed, Bassanio, than to
> Live still, and write mine epitaph.
>   (IV.1)

These words convey a kind of self-pity and resignation that detracts from Antonio's courageous acceptance of fate.

Now Gratiano, Bassanio's lightweight friend, all of whose reactions are collective, says to Shylock, "Can no prayers pierce thee?" and Shylock replies, "No, none that thou hast wit enough to make" (IV.1). It seems to me that here Shakespeare, as is his wont, slips in a hint that there was a kind of prayer that would have moved Shylock. Could we not imagine that had Antonio awakened to his own share of responsibility for the hatred in Shylock—had he been able to see and repent the enormity of his contempt over the years and to ask for *forgiveness* instead of for mercy, this would have been the piercing prayer to which Shylock would have responded? Never for an instant does Antonio acknowledge his own guilt. A turning point for many of us comes when we ask to be forgiven *by* the shadow for our failure to recognize and accept him or her: we are apt rather to concentrate on magnanimously forgiving our shadows for their iniquities. Antonio says of Shylock,

> I oft deliver'd from his forfeitures
> Many that have at times made moan to me;
> *Therefore* he hates me.
> (III.2, italics added)

These words rationalize Antonio's earlier explicit refusal to have any dealings with Shylock except as a declared enemy.

Portia, in the guise of the learned young doctor of law, with Nerissa as her clerk, now arrives and is asked by the Duke to give her opinion. Her first words are, "Which is the merchant here and which the Jew?" (IV.1). On one level, as Goddard emphasizes, this brief question may reveal to us the most profound message of the play; Antonio the virtuous merchant and the wicked Jew—are they not two sides of the same fatal human refusal of consciousness and compassion? Which indeed is which? Yet the words are also, it seems to me, revealing in another way. As Portia comes striding into court we have the impression that she does not look at either man. The question would be foolish if she used her eyes, but her attention is wholly at this moment turned upon the drama of her entrance and the fun of her disguise. She is playing one of those raw tricks she talked about. It is because we do not *look* at people as individuals that the opposites become more and more confused within us.

Portia, however, is soon now to open her heart to the tragedy of these two men as she speaks to each one and sees them for the first time. She asks Antonio if he acknowledges the bond; he answers, "I do," and suddenly she forgets the brilliant dramatic performance she is putting on and speaks straight out of her heart, transcending all the trivial superficialities of her usual environment by which the truth of her feelings were so often obscured, and reaching down to a depth of understanding of which she had not known herself capable. Perhaps it is not easy for an actress to convey the inwardness of this startling change of level—but the words proclaim it. Familiar as they are, I will quote again those great and moving lines, which stay illuminated in the memory when the excitement of the play is long past.

Portia	Then must the Jew be merciful.
Shylock	On what compulsion must I? Tell me that.
Portia	The quality of mercy is not strained.
	It droppeth as the gentle rain from heaven
	Upon the place beneath: it is twice blest;
	It blesseth him that gives and him that takes:
	'Tis mightiest in the mightiest; it becomes
	The throned monarch better than his crown;
	His sceptre shows the force of temporal power,
	The attribute to awe and majesty,
	wherein doth sit the dread and fear of kings;
	But mercy is above this scepter'd sway;
	It is enthroned in the heart of kings,
	It is an attribute to God himself;
	And earthly power doth show likest God's
	When mercy seasons justice. Therefore, Jew,
	Though justice be thy plea, consider this—
	That, in the course of justice, none of us
	Should see salvation: we do pray for mercy;
	And that same prayer doth teach us all to render
	The deeds of mercy.
	(IV.1)

The words ring out, affirming Shakespeare's greatest theme—the possibility of the transformation of power by love, which is the condition of all salvation. Portia gives Shylock a great chance before destroying him. There is in imagination here a pause—one of those silences, however brief, in which irrevocable choices are made. We must surely believe that somewhere in the darkness of his passion Shylock saw a brief light and turned from it in deliberate rejection.

> My deeds upon my head! I crave the law.
> (IV.1)

The die is cast for Shylock. But what of Portia? Will she be true to her vision of compassion, or will she return to the dramatic "tricks" she so much enjoys? She cannot at this point resist the "scepter'd sway" of her animus, and she rejects mercy and humility, which had for a moment been "enthroned" in her heart. The extreme skill of Shakespeare's dramatic power can blind people to the shocking cruelty of the way she spins out the action and, oblivious to the unnecessary torture she is inflicting on Antonio and her own beloved Bassanio, plays for a last-minute reprieve. She makes Antonio bare his breast, demands to see the weighing scales, goads Shylock into a refusal even to summon a surgeon.

In contrast to Portia's histrionics, Antonio and Bassanio show here in their degree the truth and generosity of their friendship.

Antonio	Grieve not that I am fallen to this for you. . . .
	Commend me to your honourable wife. . .
	Say how I loved you, speak me fair in death.
Bassanio	Antonio, I am married to a wife
	Which is as dear to me as life itself;
	But life itself, my wife, and all the world
	Are not with me esteem'd above thy life.
	(IV.1)

Portia responds to this cry from the heart with a witty aside and proceeds to bring the tension to breaking point by repeating twice, almost with relish,

> A pound of that same merchant's flesh is thine;
> The court awards it and the law doth give it.
> And you must cut this flesh from off his breast;
> The law allows it, and the court awards it.
> (IV.1)

Shylock raises his knife, and only then does Portia spring her trap.

> Tarry a little; there is something else.
> This bond doth give thee here no jot of blood.
> (IV.1)

Under Portia's decree that, should he shed one drop of Antonio's blood, all his property would be confiscated by the state, Shylock immediately backs off and tries to accept the money. She says he can have nothing but his bond, and turns now from tormenting her friends to an almost exultant condemnation of her fallen enemy. It is left to the Duke to show some degree of compassion. Since Shylock had planned murder through the law, his goods and life are forfeit. The Duke spares Shylock's life and assigns his goods to Antonio, but he leaves to Antonio himself the final decision.

It is Antonio's great opportunity to show the mercy that Shylock had denied to him, to disprove the accusation, "If a Jew wrong a Christian, what is his humility? Revenge." It is true that Antonio does not take all that he can from Shylock. He makes a show of magnanimity and thinks generously of providing for Jessica and her husband; but that he has had no change of heart is shockingly clear, for he ends this show of goodheartedness by the most merciless insult he could have hurled at his enemy. He makes his offer contingent on Shylock's becoming a Christian. By this he shows his contempt not only for the integrity of a man, but for the very nature of true religion.

Everything had been taken away from Antonio, as it was from Job; everything is now restored, but Antonio, unlike Job, knows no transformation in his soul. The status quo is sadly reestablished. In this production, however, at Stratford, director and actor added a single note of hope for Antonio. At the very end, after the last line was spoken and "exeunt" all the players, Jessica was left sitting by herself at the front of the stage. She alone, we were invited to imagine, had been touched to sadness by her father's plight, to which no one else gave a thought any more. Antonio, catching sight of her, turned back from the others and held out his hand to her. I have a feeling that Shakespeare would have deeply approved. Antonio is capable of touching and being touched by Jessica, if not by Shylock. It is a mere hint of a possibility, but in that hint the forgiveness and reconciliation brought to full expression so many years later in *The Tempest* is already implicit.

Portia, as we have seen, had likewise rejected her great opportunity, but much more understandably, through thoughtless immaturity rather than through a settled blindness. She is positively intoxicated with her success and proceeds in her disguise to play a cruel trick on her beloved Bassanio. She refuses any payment for having saved his friend from death and himself from a lifelong guilt, except the gift of the ring that she as his wife had given him and from which she had made him swear never to part. So follow the superficially light-hearted and amusing scenes concerning this ring. Of course she was only teasing him and always meant to forgive him, but it is the cruel teasing of the brilliant adolescent in her. We are surely meant to appreciate the irony that, having chosen to marry a man who will "give and hazard all he has," she discovers that he will also give and hazard her when the need arises!

However, there is love between Portia and Bassanio. Maggie Smith, in her television performance of the part, was particularly moving in her affirmation of this truth of Portia's heart. Bassanio is a good, true, simple, and loving fellow, purged of much self-deceit by his experience of what thoughtlessness can do to a friend. Portia in her brilliance will wind him round her little finger, but she will nevertheless love and respect him for the simplicity she lacks. He will adore her with the loyalty of his nature, and this, I like to feel, will bring kindness to her wit and maturity to her compassion as she grows to the stature of that immortal Portia who has glimpsed the "quality of mercy" and who, in the quiet pause of introversion before her reunion with Bassanio, reflects on the nature of proportion and growth:

> How many things by season season'd are
> To their right praise and true perfection!
> (V.1)

Antony and Cleopatra

Harold C. Goddard wrote, "The destiny of the world is determined less by the battles that are lost and won than by the stories it loves and believes in."[1] Antony and Cleopatra were two actual people whose lives became a source for one of the great stories of the world—a story that was retold by Shakespeare at the very height of his poetic, dramatic, and psychological powers, so that generations of playgoers and readers feel their hearts so "blown" by it that they recreate it for themselves. The word "blown" in this sense—i.e., swelled to bursting—is used in the play by Enobarbus. "This blows my heart," he exclaims as he realizes the sheer greatness of Antony and the shame of his own betrayal. His words reveal that he has suddenly become aware through real feeling of the meaning behind his actions. The image is exact: when the wind of the spirit blows into the secret corners of the heart, swelling it almost to the bursting point, a man hears his own story. Because his own heart was "blown" in this way, Enobarbus's betrayal was transformed from just another account of a weak man's failure, which would have made his former life seem a pointless series of events, to a story remaining in our memory (beside those of Antony and of Cleopatra) with its own unfading power to move us.

The first brief scene of the play contains so much that it leaves us gasping, already, as it were, in the wind. Philo describes Antony's great "captain's heart," which, he says, had swelled in battle enough to burst the buckles of his armor, and adds that this heart has now "become the bellows and the fan to cool a gypsy's lust" (I.1). Thus the story opens with these same images of wind and heart; indeed the whole play is about their interaction. Philo, the ordinary soldier, sees nothing but lust. Antony's spirit has been degraded to this: "The triple pillar of the world transformed into a strumpet's fool: behold and see." And on these words Antony appears with Cleopatra, as though we are immediately asked to judge for ourselves the truth of Philo's opinion. Antony superficially confirms it, but at the same time so lifts us beyond the limitations of such as Philo that—especially when we know the ending of the story—we feel at once the triviality of Philo's statement.

Cleopatra   If it be love indeed, tell me how much.

Antony   There's beggary in the love that can be reckon'd.

Cleopatra   I'll set a bourn how far to be beloved.

Antony   Then must thou needs find out new heaven, new earth.
(I.1)[2]

These four lines express concisely and wittily a typical approach to the psyche of a half-conscious man as opposed to that of a half-conscious woman. Antony talks in vast terms of the scope and nature of his love, while Cleopatra is obviously interested in the immediate personal situation between them, as the rest of the scene makes clear; for in spite of his talk of a new heaven and earth, she is not at all sure that his present feelings for her are strong enough to keep him at her side in defiance of his wife's demands and his loyalty to Caesar. Her doubt of his practical constancy is more than justified by events, but nevertheless his first words express a true and great intuition of that vision of a new heaven and a new earth to which both he and she will finally come—despite (or perhaps because of) all the failures and the betrayals into which they fall. Both must discover and experience defeat before they can know the love that makes all things new. There is a letter written by C. G. Jung in April 1959 to Cary Baynes in which Jung comments on the difference between men and women in their response to psychology: "It is just as if women knew less of its implications, as they know psychology chiefly as a means to an end, while a man has an incomparably more complete intuition about it although he knows very much less of it than a woman."[3] And indeed, as Jung goes on to say, often for this very reason a man evades the immediate psychological issues.

As Antony speaks the words "new heaven, new earth," a servant comes to tell him that a messenger from Rome has arrived—the representative of the political and rational world in which the passion of love has no part. The reactions of the man and the woman to this news are again typical. Antony in his dream of love refuses to see the envoy, puts off the unpleasant moment when he must look at the facts of his situation; he would like to jump over them into a false heaven which is still for him identified with pleasure.

Now, for the love of Love and her soft hours,
Let's not confound the time with conference harsh!
There's not a minute of our lives should stretch
Without some pleasure now.
　　　(I.1)

In contrast, Cleopatra, the extremely feminine and thoroughly realistic woman, urges him again and again to see the messengers. For her, for most women, her pleasure in her love will be spoiled if there is a greatly feared uncertainty in the background about her lover's faithfulness. How will he respond to messages from his wife and from Caesar, who, she knows, will summon him to leave her to fulfill his duty in Rome? She taunts him with her wholly personal anxiety, and once again he replies with that double note—an unrealistic evasion of fact combined with the sublime poetry of an intuitive truth.

Let Rome in Tiber melt, and the wide arch
Of the ranged empire fall! Here is my space.
Kingdoms are clay!
　　　(I.1)

He embraces Cleopatra and adds, "The nobleness of life is to do thus; when such a mutual pair and such a twain can do't" (I.1). It is no ordinary lustful embrace, for he knows they are capable of realizing together the nothingness of worldly power in the presence of love. What he does not realize is that a man's full debt to his work in the world must be paid and the conflict endured to the end before he may say, "Here is my space."

As for Cleopatra, she too proves at the outset the superficiality of Philo's description of her love as nothing but a wanton's lust. Of course, audiences have already an image of Cleopatra in their minds before the play opens—her name has for centuries evoked the fascinating "she" whose power to ensnare men is almost irresistible, the greatest *femme fatale* of history. A true actress, such as Maggie Smith this year, will immediately convey in this first scene the power of Cleopatra's fascination and will make it very clear that her charm is *not* that of the mere wanton arousing only lust. Indeed, how could so crude an attraction of the flesh alone enslave such a man as Antony?

It is true that here at the beginning Cleopatra has no inkling of her own capacity for the new heaven and earth of a single love, but it is immediately apparent, as is usual in women, that her feeling for Antony is at this point much less physically lustful than his. She does not seem interested in the immediate pleasures he talks about; on the contrary, her emotion is seen all through the early scene as an intense possessiveness on the psychic level. She wants to absorb his attention, to be assured that she has no rival of any kind, to be told over and over again how much *he* loves *her*. Her very first line, "If it be love indeed, tell me how much," is very familiar indeed to women, and many men have been exasperated beyond measure by a woman's constant need for verbal reassurance that she is loved. Very often she senses a fundamental conflict such as Antony's in the man she loves, and fails to accept the necessity for sacrifice, which is the *sine qua non* of that love which is a free bond and to which a man or woman is unconditionally committed. He still confuses love with pleasure, while in her it is a demand for emotional domination. She proceeds with the usual tricks half-consciously designed to goad Antony into subjection; she taunts him with her jealousy of Fulvia, his wife, and her fear of Caesar's influence. She is full of contradictions; knowing him to be listening at last to the messengers, she is driven by her fear. She wants to see him, she hides herself when he comes; she will be merry, she says, when he is sad, sad when he is merry; obsessed with the thought of the absent Fulvia's influence, she cannot even let him get a word in to tell her he has heard of his wife's death. When she finally hears this, she blames him for his lack of sorrow, for his faithlessness, which shows how easily he will leave *her* and forget his love, and so on. In fact, she exhibits all the most tiresome traits of the possessive female. "Can Fulvia die?" she cries, intuiting somehow that it is not the actual Fulvia that separates her from Antony, but a far more dangerous inner split in him and in herself.

Yet as the act goes on we begin to penetrate behind these frantic demands to the greatness of the Queen, and we glimpse the warmth and generosity of her royal nature. Suddenly she emerges from her pettiness, accepting that he must indeed go to Rome; and her words—which are often read as further comic taunting of Antony, but which need not be so—reveal that she is shocked into a bewildered recognition that there is something in her love so great, so unknowable, that she is for once bereft of words.

> Courteous lord, one word.
> Sir, you and I must part, but that's not it:
> Sir, you and I have loved, but there's not it:
> That you know well: something it is I would,—
> O, my oblivion is a very Antony,
> And I am all forgotten.
> (I.3)

As I read the lines, she is groping after her own soul, which is living in him; and then in truth she does forget herself for a moment and her objective love is first heard.

> Your honor calls you hence;
> Therefore be deaf to my unpitied folly,
> And all the gods go with you!
> (I.3)

And Antony is also lifted for a brief moment beyond his conflict.

> Our separation so abides and flies
> That thou, residing here, go'st yet with me,
> And I, hence fleeting, here remain with thee.
> (I.3)

She may fall into nagging, he into political dishonesties, but their royalty, their individual stature shines from the beginning through it all. He says of her:

> Fie, wrangling queen!
> Whom everything becomes, to chide, to laugh,
> To weep; whose every passion fully strives
> To make itself, in thee, fair and admired.
> (I.1)

And she of him:

> O Charmian,
> Where thinkst thou he is now?
> Stands he, or sits he?
> Or does he walk? Or is he on his horse?
> O happy horse, to bear the weight of Antony!
> Do bravely, horse! For wott'st thou whom thou movest?
> The demi-Atlas of this earth, the arm
> And burgonet of men.
>> (I.5)

Burgonet means helmet. Antony is to her that which supports and protects the whole world by his thought and action.

There is somehow no pettiness even in their most easily despised weaknesses because of the essential *singleness* of their vision of each other —a total devotion which is at the same time never exclusive. They love and are loved by their friends and servants through all their humiliations and follies to the ultimate defeat. This is the test of integrity in love.

The other two "pillars of the world"—Octavius Caesar and Lepidus—are now revealed. Through their first words on the stage Shakespeare again sums up the essence of each man. Caesar is still very young, but he is portrayed as an immensely able, cold, and calculating ruler, who is rapidly becoming incapable of allowing his heart to influence his head.

> You may see, Lepidus, and henceforth know,
> It is not Caesar's natural vice to hate
> Our great competitor. From Alexandria
> This is the news: he fishes, drinks, and wastes
> The lamps of night in revel: is not more manlike
> Than Cleopatra, nor the Queen of Ptolemy
> More womanly than he: hardly gave audience, or
> Vouchsafed to think he had partners: you shall find there
> A man who is the abstract of all faults
> That all men follow.
>> (I.4)

No, it is not natural vice that threatened Octavius Caesar; perhaps if he could have let himself hate naturally he would also have discovered that he could love. These few words hint at the identification of Octavius and all his natural emotions with Caesar, the lover of power. He is therefore contemptuous of all the sins of the flesh that so often accompany largeness of heart in a man of Antony's stature—condemning them as "womanly." All feminine qualities are for him despicable weaknesses. A man, he says, who can put a woman before the support of Caesar is beneath contempt. Later we are told that Antony easily weeps when moved, like a woman. I am reminded of Winston Churchill weeping over the devastation of London. Caesar, who by his pompous rejection of his "natural vices" has turned his back on his potential individuation, says of Antony, who has entered with his whole heart into the torment of warring instincts, that he is an "*abstract*" of all faults that all men follow." The description fits Caesar perfectly, for he is indeed an "abstract" of those qualities that attract the herd through self-interest.

Caesar, having achieved his goals and eliminated his rivals, is later described with penetrating accuracy as "the universal landlord." No phrase could better illuminate his quality as compared with the royalty of spirit in Antony and Cleopatra, which shines through defeat and death. Landlords may be just or unjust, administering their possessions fairly or shamelessly exploiting them, but their power is more and more an impersonal abstraction to their tenants, the larger their possessions become. The "*universal*" landlord implies the remote absentee owner, cut off from any personal relationship with the tenants, while the images of King and Queen in the psyche involve depths of symbolic feeling and responsibility towards each individual subject. However necessary landlords are in society, the great majority of the stories (particularly fairy stories) that have sprung up from and nourished the unconscious of man are concerned with kings and princes, queens and princesses—for we must know the inborn royalty of the Self if we are to find ourselves as free individuals.

Caesar continues to lay bare his egocentricity and poverty of heart. Answering Lepidus's efforts to be nice to everybody, he announces that while all kinds of drunkenness and debauchery are entirely natural and to be condoned in the ordinary way, yet since Antony's "lightness" forces him, Caesar, to carry an extra weight of care, Antony's actions are inexcusable. Sextus Pompeius, son of the great Pompey, has risen in rebellion and threatens the power of the triumvirate, and Antony, the greatest fighter of them all, has neglected his duty—namely, to help Caesar. Therefore his behavior is shameful.

We listen to more cynical hypocrisy, this time from Pompey, for whom likewise things are good or bad according to whether or not they contribute to his power. "If the great gods be just, they shall assist the deeds of justest men." He will be successful because of the wickedness of his opponents—a very familiar argument. He sums up his enemies crisply in a few lines:

> Mark Antony
> In Egypt sits at dinner and will make
> No wars without doors. Caesar gets money where
> He loses hearts: Lepidus flatters them both,
> Of both is flatter'd, but he neither loves
> Nor either cares for him.
>   (II.1)

Neither Caesar nor Pompey gives any value to personal love; their concern is with the attachment of the public to themselves. Marriage is a political convenience, as when Caesar coldly uses his sister as a bid for Antony's support; and all other devotion to a woman is simply lust to be indulged as long as it is no threat to power. At this point Jung's words about love and power are peculiarly apt: "What can love mean to a man with a hunger for power: that is why we always find two main causes of psychic catastrophes; on the one hand a disappointment with love and on the other hand a thwarting of the striving for power." The situation is ripe for catastrophe. The three "pillars of the world" are now seen together: Lepidus is fussily telling everyone to speak gently; Caesar accuses Antony of breaking his oath by failing to support him in his wars; Antony with admirable generosity of heart admits his negligence, but affirms his honor. Then one of Caesar's friends proposes that a marriage between Antony and Caesar's sister Octavia would be "an unslipping knot" binding the two rulers together. The proposal, it is obvious, has been well thought out beforehand and craftily produced at the critical moment, as though it were a new idea to Caesar.

Now Antony commits his real sin, betraying his commitment to the emerging truth of his feeling: he is invaded by his shadow's love of power, personified in Caesar, and, knowing he has been guilty of irresponsibility, he tells himself that all his emotional experiences have been nothing but lust. Nevertheless, though disastrously and half-consciously blind to Caesar's cynical bargaining with his sister's life and happiness, Antony is not coldly hypocritical. He has the usual weakness of those whose largeness of heart is as yet undiscriminating and undisciplined, and he credits Caesar with his own ingenuousness.

> Let me have thy hand:
> Further this act of grace; and from this hour
> The heart of brothers govern in our loves
> And sway our great designs!
> (II.2)

He is deluded into the belief that love can be ignited and used in the service of power to produce good ends. Caesar is a boy in years but old already in the realm of political manipulation; Antony is gray-haired but comparatively a child on the emotional level and therefore at Caesar's mercy. Such unconscious ingenuousness can lead to the infliction of great suffering on others, all with the best intentions. This is Antony's real sin; but it is the kind of sin that in the generous heart may lead through suffering to love. Caesar's kind of sin leads steadily away from the hope of grace.

Enobarbus is introduced to us in this scene. He is Antony's most devoted friend and lieutenant, clear-eyed, discriminating, and outspoken, full of wit and feeling—a man, in fact, such as Shakespeare loved to honor. Not for a moment is he deluded, like his master, by the fine sentiments everyone is pouring out. He divines at once that this marriage will cause a far worse rift between Caesar and Antony than any that is already in existence, because he knows his master and friend in all his weaknesses and strengths; and moreover he knows Cleopatra and has recognized in her the spellbinding power and beauty of the woman and the queen. There is poetic vision in the down-to-earth Enobarbus. Here in part is his famous description of her first appearance to him and to Mark Antony and its effect.

> The barge she sat in, like a burnished throne,
> Burn'd on the water. The poop was beaten gold;
> Purple the sails and so perfumed that
> The winds were love-sick with them; the oars were silver,
> Which to the tune of flutes kept stroke, and made
> The water which they beat to follow faster,
> As amorous of their strokes. For her own person,
> It beggar'd all description.
> (II.2)

The rich colors, the gold and silver, entrance the eye; the sound of music enslaves the waters; the delicacy of scent fills the air so that the very winds are in love; and through the winds the enchantment reaches the shore and enters the hearts of all the people of Cleopatra's city.

> From the barge
> A strange invisible perfume hits the sense
> Of the adjacent wharfs. The city cast
> Her people out upon her; and Antony,
> Enthron'd i' the market-place, did sit alone,
> Whistling to the air; which, but for vacancy,
> Had gone to gaze on Cleopatra too,
> And made a gap in nature.
> (II.2)

As Enobarbus tells it, Cleopatra, refusing Antony's invitation to supper, makes him *her* guest.

> Our courteous Antony
> Whom ne'er the word of "No" woman heard speak
> Being barber'd ten times o'er, goes to the feast
> And, for his ordinary, pays his heart
> For what his eyes eat only.
> (II.2)

Enobarbus knows, as none of the others do, that it is not just a matter of sexual appetite, for the Cleopatra he describes is the eternal goddess in the unconscious of the man—Enobarbus has a vision of beauty and has glimpsed that which is beyond and behind all desire.

Agrippa makes a crude comment. Enobarbus, obviously lost in his own vision, does not even hear. He goes on:

> I saw her once
> Hop forty paces through the public street;
> And having lost her breath, she spoke and panted,
> That she did make defect perfection,
> And, breathless, power breathe forth.
> (II.2)

"Now Antony must leave her utterly," says Maecenas. And Enobarbus replies with prophetic certainty, "Never, he will not." And then he speaks those immortal words about Cleopatra, which we may remember whenever we encounter those rare individual people in life or in story who awaken the imagination and through whom life pours into all around them: "Age cannot wither her, nor custom stale her infinite variety" (II.2). We may find such persons among the wise, among artists or actresses (surely Maggie Smith is one of them), or indeed among the outcasts of society. Thus Enobarbus knew that for Antony to reject Cleopatra for long was a virtual impossibility.

> For vilest things
> Become themselves in her, that the holy priests
> Bless her when she is riggish.
> (II.2)

Conventional codes of morality are simply irrelevant in the face of such a torrent of life.

Maecenas, still totally uncomprehending, reflects hopefully that Octavia's beauty, wisdom, and modesty may settle Antony's heart. What chance has her cool, gentle, and obedient quality against that "infinite variety"? Antony says in all good faith to Octavia, "I have not kept my square, but that to come shall all be done by the rule" (II.3). As well try to confine a hurricane in a box as expect Antony to act "by the rule." We realize how little Antony understands himself.

Immediately following this scene of dutiful obtuseness the odd figure of the Soothsayer arrives—a voice from the unconscious trying to
break through Antony's fog and bring him to some awareness, just as a
powerful dream may shock us after some particular fall into compla-
cency. The Soothsayer speaks the warning of the unconscious: "Hie you
to Egypt again." He tells Antony that he will be destroyed if he does not
separate himself from Caesar—and all that Caesar stands for—as quickly as possible.

> Thy daemon, that thy spirit which keeps thee, is
> Noble, courageous, high, unmatchable,
> Where Caesar's is not; but near him thy angel
> Becomes a fear, as being o'erpow'r'd: therefore
> Make space enough between you.
>
> If thou dost play with him at any game,
> Thou art sure to lose; and of that natural luck
> He beats thee 'gainst the odds. Thy lustre thickens
> When he shines by. I say again, thy spirit
> Is all afraid to govern thee near him,
> But, he away, 'tis noble.
>   (II.3)

Could there be any more acute psychological observation than is contained in these lines? You cannot play games and make compromises
with the shadow. A man who is split, who is untrue to his daemon, to
his own fateful truth, is bound to lose at any worldly game. The successful gambler is nearly always the one who is already rich. The man
who is ruthlessly determined on winning power or riches will have all
the "luck" because he is undivided and without fear in his particular
quest. Those who are wholly devoted to one thing only will have either
the "luck of the devil" or that other rare kind of fortune which has been
called "holy luck," according to the nature of that to which they devote
themselves. This one-pointedness is an attribute of greatness in all fields
of human endeavor. The greatest leaders of men, for instance, such as
Napoleon, Wellington, and Churchill, were never touched by bullet or
sword, though they constantly exposed themselves to danger. They sim-

ply ignored danger as irrelevant to them personally. This was also said of Antony.

Antony does not listen with real understanding to the Soothsayer. He hears the superficial meaning but not the wisdom. He knows the man is right about Caesar's luck, so he thinks to himself he'll go back to Egypt for "his pleasure," without giving up his compromise with Caesar. As so often when the unconscious speaks and we don't listen, our case, as was Antony's, is worse than before. He decides to play the outer game for a while with Octavia and Caesar, and to go back to Cleopatra when it suits him. In other words, he wants to have his cake and eat it too. Far from making space enough between himself and his Caesar shadow, he is now inwardly much more dominated by him. His ego has indeed become for the moment possessed by the shadow, as is inevitable when we try to have it both ways, and his daemon, his individual spirit, his angel, is eclipsed, leaving him in fear and uncertainty, disastrously split.

Meanwhile, in Alexandria, a messenger brings news to Cleopatra of Antony's marriage, just as she is enjoying memories of her power over him. She, like Antony, is blinded by her power-driven shadow, the highly emotional personal possessiveness of woman. She even projects her fury onto the unfortunate messenger, striking him, sending him away, calling him back and asking for more and more details of her rival. There is however a single moment in the midst of all this when the daemon of Cleopatra, *her* spirit of clear discrimination and justice, stops the flood of emotion.

> These hands do lack nobility, that they strike
> A meaner than myself, since I myself
> Have given myself the cause.
> (II.5)

The voice of the hidden angel speaks to her out of the fire of her anger, and she sees for a moment the futility of projecting her miseries. "I myself have given myself the cause"—a phrase for all to remember in the midst of even mildly hurt feelings.

Act II ends with the scene on board Pompey's ship, where he entertains the three "pillars of the world" to celebrate their peace pact. The whole lot of them are extremely drunk, except Caesar, who disapproves of it all, being drunk himself in a far worse way on the "spirits" of power. Antony urges him to enjoy himself, saying, "Be a child o' the time," to which Caesar replies, "*Possess* it, I'll make answer" (II.7). "Instinct and intellect" (Dante), "blood and judgment" (Hamlet) are at war in the rulers of the world; all are therefore driven by unconscious forces, as are all drunken men. Only Enobarbus remains objective. The deeper note is very easily missed in so many of Shakespeare's seemingly superficial exchanges. For instance, "They are his shards (wings) and he their beetle" (III.2) says Enobarbus, speaking of Lepidus. The other two are for Lepidus the "wings" that lift him out of his mediocrity—his collective "beetle" nature—whereas for Caesar and Antony the false feeling and flattery of Lepidus are at the crawling heart of their fine protestations of love and friendship. Immediately after these words are spoken, we are given proof of their truth. Antony and the unhappy Octavia are saying goodbye to Caesar, and the two rulers affirm vehemently their brotherly love and fidelity to each other as they use the gentleness of Octavia to further their ends. Neither has as yet any consciousness of value in the feeling realm. Under the wings of their words the hidden beetle has already begun to eat through that "unslipping knot."

Octavia and Antony go to Athens, but very soon the truth comes into the open. Octavia is miserably torn in half. Antony complains bitterly of Caesar's betrayals: Caesar has broken the pact with Pompey; he has used Lepidus and then arrested him on trumped-up charges; and moreover Antony declares it intolerable that Caesar is steadily undermining the reputation in Rome of Antony himself. These charges may all be true, but they have the flavor of a determined rationalization of Antony's longing for Egypt. Octavia offers to go to Rome as mediator, and when she arrives is greeted by her brother with the news that Antony has returned to Egypt in her absence, where, says Caesar, "He hath given his empire up to a whore" (III.4). He exhorts Octavia to cheer up and affirms that she is very dear to him. Indeed she is dearer than ever, since Antony's treatment of her has given him a new and "righteous" cause. It is plain that he is now so sure of himself, having eliminated the threat from Pompey and the nuisance of Lepidus, that he is delighted to be able to fight Antony openly and so achieve supreme dictatorship for himself alone. He rationalizes his motives of power just as Antony rationalized his feelings.

It is true of course that Antony has treated Octavia shamefully—as he had also, in fact, treated Cleopatra—and he will have to pay for these betrayals of feeling by a terrible fall into the unconscious and a defeat in the outer world, which together almost destroy him and the meaning of his life. Jung said once, "If you feel yourself falling, jump." Because at the last Antony does not *fall* but consciously embraces his fate and accepts his darkness, he is not lost but carried by those disasters to the new heaven and new earth, which, as he had intuited at the very beginning, lay hidden in the boundlessness of his love.

We come now to the dispute between Antony and all his best advisors about whether to fight Caesar on sea or on land. These are symbolic meanings that are clear to us in our time. By his determination to fight by sea he proves that his undifferentiated emotions are driving him to choose a battle in the realm of the unconscious where he still believes himself to be in control and where he will not need to separate from his beloved or from his own anima. Cleopatra urges the sea battle because she will then be able to stay near him through the fighting, in one of her ships. She is also trying to ape the masculine qualities she adores in Antony instead of exercising her own discrimination. Enobarbus points this out to Cleopatra very clearly. She replies, "A charge we bear i' the war, and, as the president of my kingdom, will appear there for a man" (III.7). Enobarbus knows how she will merely cloud the clear judgment of the man emotionally tied to her. All women of high intelligence are faced with this easy delusion in our time. Many fall by saying "I have a charge, a responsibility, to the world, I will appear there as a man," because they will not face a conscious relationship to their inner masculinity. The true responsibility of woman in such a case is to appear on the battlefield of the world not "for a man" but as a woman with her gift of penetration into the true feeling values of every conflict, which the purely masculine urge to achievement so easily tramples down. Antony is advised to fight on land by all his friends and advisors and even by a simple soldier from the ranks with earthy common sense. Enobarbus tells Antony to think of the poor quality of his ships and the lack of experience of their crews. The soldier says emotionally, "We have used to conquer, standing on the earth and fighting foot to foot." Shakespeare emphasizes the almost somnambulistic way in which Antony replies to all of them: "By sea, by sea. . . . I'll fight at sea" (III.7). He will not fight standing on the earth of reality; he cannot hear the warning, either of reason or of intuition.

The hand of fate is in all this; he is about to learn that he is not master in his house; that the "sea" can swallow up all his sureness of judgment—even his honor and his courage. At the height of the battle Cleopatra orders her ship to turn and fly for home, and to the amazement and horror of all who know him, Antony, whose courage in battle is legendary, turns his own ship and sails after Cleopatra, away from the enemy, in a fever of anxiety, as though tied to her by an unbreakable thread—as indeed he is. This is indeed the truly "unslipping knot" in his life, only to be untied when he is ready voluntarily and consciously to tie it in the final commitment of death. At this point Antony is still far from knowing Cleopatra as a true human woman. He calls her Thetis (the sea goddess). He is in the grip of the archetype of woman within— the goddess of the depths. He and all his conscious strength must be swallowed up if he is to come to rebirth. By all outer standards, how wrong he was to fight by sea! Yet how right it was that the myth behind his life, even though it was as yet dangerously unconscious, forced him through the darkness to his great opportunity and produced so great a story for the world. "We have kiss'd away kingdoms and provinces" (III.10) say his friends, watching his navy's defeat. Yes indeed, but Antony will finally know a kiss to be worth more than them all.

Goddard has pointed out that in spite of the greatness of Shakespeare's dramatic and poetic achievement in *Antony and Cleopatra,* it has not competed with the four famous tragedies—*Hamlet, Othello, Macbeth,* and *King Lear*—in the affections of men and women, and he suggests that the reason for this "seems to be that Antony and Cleopatra, compared with Shakespeare's other heroes and heroines, even the Macbeths, are a pair soiled and stained by long submersion in the world." This means that Antony and Cleopatra are not "great" in the simple sense that Othello and King Lear are great both in their darkness and their light; nor are they great in evil like Macbeth and his wife, nor great as highly sensitive artists and intellectuals caught in neurotic conflict, in the manner of Hamlet. Antony and Cleopatra are very much more like all of us in their ordinary human virtues, vices, and emotions, swayed by anger, fear, vanity, possessiveness, and by courage, generosity, duty, and a longing to love and be loved. We may be more simply and profoundly moved by contemplating the good and evil portrayed in such figures as King Lear or Macbeth—yet *Antony and Cleopatra* carries a special meaning, for in it lies the intensity with which they live their emotional lives. They are wholehearted, even in their little defects, their absurd lovers' touchiness, their vanities and jealousies, and it is as though Shakespeare uncovers for us the truth that whatever we are and however often we fall, if we live every moment with that kind of devotion to what *is,* then the experience of transformation, even if it does not come until the moment of death, will be equally intense and all-embracing.

Having awakened from the dream in which he had moved during the sea battle, Antony is plunged into a state of remorse, or rather repentance, in which he makes no excuses and evades nothing of the consequences.

> Hark! the land bids me tread no more upon't;
> It is ashamed to bear me. Friends, come hither.
> I am so lated in the world that I
> Have lost my way for ever. I have a ship
> Laden with gold; take that, divide it; fly,
> And make your peace with Caesar.
> (III.11)

Here is his simple humanity—his thought is always for his friends as soon as he is aware of himself again—his "noble, unmatchable" spirit rises again, and a beautiful and moving scene with Cleopatra follows. He sits brooding on his shame when she comes to him.

> *Cleopatra* O my lord, my lord,
> Forgive my fearful sails! I little thought
> You would have followed.
> *Antony*   Egypt, thou knew'st too well
> My heart was to thy rudder tied by the strings,
> And thou should'st tow me after. . . .
>
> . . .
>
> *Cleopatra*   O, my pardon!
> (III.11)

Antony faces the fact of his humiliation before the young man, Caesar, and then turns to Cleopatra.

Fall not a tear, I say; one of them rates
All that is won and lost. Give me a kiss;
Even this repays me.
(III.11)

The light shines through clearly and simply for a moment, but both of
them have yet far to go before the final vision. The ups and downs con-
tinue to the very end—for, as Goddard says, they suffer from their long
immersion in the world and its values.

A new character emerges in this little scene (III.11)—and he surely
carries an important meaning. He is Eros—Antony's armor bearer. He
appears briefly in a conversation with Enobarbus at the beginning of act
III, but now his inner significance begins to reach us. It is he who urges
Cleopatra to break through Antony's despair and comfort him, and it is
no accident that his name is Eros. Shakespeare obliquely tells us that
Antony now has a new body servant who is a mediator to him of the values of individual feeling—as indeed Eros proves himself to be from this
point to the end. Later we learn that he had been a slave and was now
set free to be a friend and willing servant.

Once again, faced with the realities of the world of collective values
in which Caesar lives, Antony reacts with the naïve simplicity of a boy.
He, the veteran warrior, actually challenges to single combat the young
man who is so secure in his immense power. The clear-thinking Enobarbus comments:

That he should dream,
Knowing all measures, the full Caesar will
Answer his emptiness! Caesar, thou hast subdued
His judgment too.
(III.13)

In one sense, this is certainly true. It is childish of Antony to expect
Caesar to meet him man to man—and yet somehow we may feel it to
be on another level a symbol of the values by which Antony is finally
governed and not simply a regression to the infantile. For, however
unrealistic, his gesture affirms an unconscious recognition that the ultimate solution of every conflict is to be found only in the individual.
They would confront each other alone and unprotected, each affirming

his unique strength, which, if it could have been seen as an inner truth, would have meant that he was ready to confront his own shadow and take full responsibility for it. To this he will come, but not yet.

Meanwhile, Caesar merely laughs at him and sends a messenger to flatter and trick Cleopatra. It is hard to understand that any critics have seen Cleopatra as a self-seeking wanton, plotting to save her own skin and to flatter Caesar. It seems to me that in this scene and in all her later dealings with him, though she is plainly a clever realist, meeting his patent deceit with outer acceptance of his power and of her necessary submission to it, there is always an ironic undercurrent. (Maggie Smith made this abundantly clear. The one word "O" spoken by her in answer to Caesar's assertion that of course her "love" for Antony was due to her fear of him was full of her sarcastic contempt for this scheme.) Cleopatra recognizes Caesar's lies and his total misunderstanding of the nature of her devotion to Antony. That she is fundamentally true to her feeling seems to me never to be in doubt. Nevertheless she can't resist a mild flirtation, and when the messenger wants to kiss her hand she allows it, with obvious pleasure at her enduring power to catch a man, at which point Antony arrives and, touched on the raw where it most hurts, descends into a positive fury with the envoy and with Cleopatra, having the former whipped and taunting her with her past loves: "Though you can guess what temperance should be, you know not what it is" (III.13). What an example of projection at its blindest! Antony is a man whose lack of temperance in all his dealings has brought him to the extreme of humiliation, and now, losing all control, he eases his pain by this wildly intemperate outburst against another. Incidentally, at this stage his moods show themselves as even more irrational and possessive than Cleopatra's emotional storms at the beginning of the play. He is going through the fire on the way to the discovery of feeling, while she is learning the true discrimination which cannot make any compromise at all with truth.

Like all their quarrels, it is very quickly made up, and Antony veers over to another extreme of desperate courage and determination to renew the fight with his dwindling armies. Again, as usual, he calls for an evening of feasting and gaiety.

Antony   Come,
          Let's have one other gaudy night. Call to me

> All my sad captains; fill our bowls; once more
> Let's mock the midnight bell.

Cleopatra It is my birthday.
> I had thought t'have held it poor; but since my lord
> Is Antony again, I will be Cleopatra.
> (III.13)

Yes, they are themselves again, throwing themselves with their usual abandon into every moment of their way and moving fast now towards their royal deaths.

Act IV is Antony's. At the beginning, the quality which, as we have seen, redeems all his excesses, rises to greatness. He speaks to his servants and takes them one by one by the hand. "I wish I could be made of so many men, and all of you clapp'd up together in an Antony, that I might do you service so good as you have done" (IV.2). In a brief scene (IV.3) we now listen to the common soldiers on guard. It is the eve of the battle. We hear that there are strange rumors abroad, and they talk among themselves, bolstering their hopes of victory. Suddenly they hear music coming from they know not where. One soldier thinks it is in the air, another that it is under the earth. They are uneasy, superstitious; it is an omen from the gods. "Is't not strange?" "Tis strange."

The unconscious is strongly activated at such fateful moments in the lives of men. Wild rumors fly around. I remember such rumors at moments of great fear in World Wars I and II, and visions are seen, such as that of the angels at Mons. Music is heard by the simple soldiers of Antony's army. Is it not a hint of the coming opportunities for the triumph of Eros over the gods of power? For music is the language of feeling. In contrast to this is the atmosphere in the opposing camp of the man of power (IV.6). "Our will is Antony be took alive," Caesar says, already anticipating the enjoyment of leading Antony and Cleopatra in chains behind his triumphal chariot in Rome. "The time of universal peace is near." Such is the cry of all the totalitarian dictators of the world. "Plant those that have revolted in the van [i.e.,vanguard], that Antony may seem to spend his fury upon himself" (IV.6).

After this meanness comes another instance of the rare generosity of Antony's spirit. Eros and Cleopatra have helped Antony into his armor—itself another moving index that his safety now depends entirely on his fidelity to his truth of feeling. And now, just before the battle, the news is brought to him that Enobarbus, his most trusted friend, has left him for Caesar. Yet, shocked as he is, he speaks no word of personal censure or resentment. Enobarbus has left his treasure behind, and Antony responds:

> Go, Eros, send his treasure after; do it;
> Detain no jot, I charge thee. Write to him—
> I will subscribe—gentle adieus and greetings;
> Say that I wish he never find more cause
> To change a master. O, my fortunes have
> Corrupted honest men! Eros, dispatch.
>   (IV.5)

His servant, Eros, is his messenger; the god Eros is alive in his heart. This man, who has come to his last battle and knows it, whose need of true friends is at its greatest, yet feels no bitterness, will exact no payment at all. He is obviously deeply hurt, but sad, not angry at the corruption, blaming it on his own misfortunes, for which he has already recognized his responsibility. It is a scene to move one to tears.

Moreover, the creative effect on others of such unconditional forgiveness is incalculable; it literally saves Enobarbus from that worst of sins, the betrayal of a friend, for he is forced into self-knowledge by Antony's response. "O Antony, thou mine of bounty," he cries. "This blows my heart" (IV.6). He will die rather than fight against this man who acts like a god. His temporary corruption by the rational calculations of his excellent brain and his repression of his feelings is over; and he will pay the price of full awareness. In his case it is implied that his heart is so "blown," so enlarged by the sudden influx of all that to which he has denied validity, that it breaks, and he simply dies.

The battle begins on land, and Antony is, on this first day, successful. His jubilation is great, and his expression of gratitude to his chief captain, Scarus, again touches us. Cleopatra exclaims, "Lord of lords! O infinite virtue, comest thou smiling from the world's great snare uncaught?" (IV.8). They rejoice together, and their hope of keeping both their power and their love without loss revives in another burst of somewhat feverish celebration, for both really know it is unreal.

However, they are individuals of such resolute, unwavering quality that they cannot turn their backs on "the world's great snare," either by escaping or by letting themselves be caught. On one level or another, they must turn and voluntarily embrace death.

On the following day Caesar again lures Antony to fight by sea. This time Antony watches from the land and sees his ships yield voluntarily to the enemy and go over to Caesar's side (IV.12). Immediately, and for the last time, Antony, in his despair, loses all clarity of judgment and furiously accuses Cleopatra herself of having betrayed him; the "sea," which has brought about the end of his worldly power, closes over his head. His fury pours out in tremendous lines of invective and reproach.

> Betray'd I am.
> O this false soul of Egypt! this grave charm,
> Whose eye beck'd forth my wars and call'd them home;
> Whose bosom was my crownet, my chief end,
> Like a right gypsy, hath, at fast and loose
> Beguil'd me to the very heart of loss—
> What, Eros, Eros!
> (IV.12)

As Cleopatra, appalled, leaves him, he continues:

> 'Tis well th'art gone,
> If it be well to live; but better 'twere
> Thou fell'st into my fury, for one death
> Might have prevented many—Eros, ho!
> (IV.12)

Three times he calls for Eros to be the instrument of his vengeance; but Eros does not answer. Neither will the god Eros ever come at the bidding of anyone who calls on him to destroy in another that which he will not see as his own.

Cleopatra, in despair, accused falsely of a plot, resorts, as women often do, to a plot of another kind. In order to convince Antony of her loyalty, she sends him a message that she has killed herself and has died with his name on her lips.

Antony's fury is spent. Eros is with him again as he faces complete disillusionment, describing himself as one whose image is like the shapes we see in the clouds, forever dissolving into some other form. All his proud achievements in the world are nothing but vapor; his heart, his innermost spirit, which he had given into the keeping of the one he most loved, had been despised and betrayed. So he believes. Thus stripped and naked, at last he faces death.

When Cleopatra's messenger comes telling of her death for his sake, Antony has just said in the blindness of despair, "Nay, weep not, gentle Eros; there is left us ourselves to end ourselves" (IV.14). After the renewal of his faith in his love, death remains, as it was before, the only possible goal remaining to him—but this death is not an end but the gateway to a life transformed. Instead of "There is [nothing] left us [but] ourselves to end ourselves," bringing meaningless despair, his words now vibrate with the healing of sudden rebirth. A breath of great tragedy touches us, carrying the joy of death when it is known as the crown of life:

> Unarm, Eros; the long day's task is done,
> And we must sleep. . . .
>
> . . .
>
> Off, pluck off:
> The sevenfold shield of Ajax cannot keep
> The battery from my heart. O, cleave, my sides!
> Heart, once be stronger than thy continent,
> Crack thy frail case! Apace, Eros, apace!
> No more a soldier. Bruised pieces, go;
> You have been nobly borne.
>   (IV.14)

He does not see his life any longer as a meaningless vapor without substance. He is stripped of his armor, of his outer shell, and even for that bruised covering he has respect; but that which is inside the protecting armor, inside the power struggle of his outer life, dwelling in his heart of hearts, is released into love.

> I will o'ertake thee, Cleopatra and
> Weep for my pardon. . . .
>
> . . .

> Eros!—I come, my queen.—Eros! stay for me. . . .
> . . .
> Come, Eros, Eros!
> (IV.14)

To this call Eros comes. And now Antony discovers a final and most humbly admitted weakness in himself.

> I, that with my sword
> Quarter'd the world, and o'er green Neptune's back
> With ships made cities, condemn myself to lack
> The courage of a woman; less noble mind
> Than she which by her death our Caesar tells,
> "I am conqueror of myself."
> (IV.14)

He, the great conqueror, cannot at the last conquer himself, cannot, that is, take his own life. He asks his servant to plunge the sword into him. Eros, the simple human servant, teaches his master the meaning of the god Eros in the human soul. The final act of self-surrender must be a wholly conscious act for which a man must take full and lonely responsibility. No one can do it for him, even if asked; nor can he, if he seeks the light, leave it to some half-consciously invited accident or happening or disease to determine the *final* moment of going. Someone told me recently of a man close to him who had lain for some time in a coma and who in lucid intervals spoke of a door that periodically opened and closed again. He said that he must, he knew, willingly *choose* to go through the door. He had not done so and that was why it closed again. Soon afterwards he quietly died. He had chosen to cross the threshold.[4]

> Eros   My dear master,
> My captain, and my emperor, let me say,
> Before I strike this bloody stroke, farewell.
> (IV.14)

So speaks Eros and kills not his master but himself.

Antony   Thrice nobler than myself!
Thou teachest me, O valiant Eros, what
I should, and thou couldst not. My queen and Eros
Have, by their brave instruction, got upon me
A nobleness on record: but I will be
A bridegroom in my death, and run into't
As to a lover's bed. Come, then; and Eros,
Thy master dies thy scholar: to do thus
I learn'd of thee.
                    (IV.14)

He makes his choice in final humility. He falls on his sword, but his life
is not yet complete, and so the blade does not kill at once. He calls his
guards; and now comes another messenger from Cleopatra to tell him
the truth; she has realized what her lie might do to Antony. "I am come,
I dread, too late" (IV.14) the messenger cries. "Too late" in his eyes is in
fact a perfect timing, as Antony surely knows. He begs to be taken at
once to his beloved. There is a quietness in him now as he tries to comfort his sorrowing guards.

Take me up,
I have led you oft; carry me now, good friends,
And have my thanks for all.
                    (IV.14)

Even the greatest must be carried at the end, by those who have been the
followers. He is brought to Cleopatra's monument, where she has taken
refuge and is in great distress. No word of reproach for Cleopatra's lie
passes his lips. It is as though he knows the ultimate integrity of her
being before she has realized it herself. "O, Antony, Antony, Antony,"
she cries—and he replies:

Peace!
Not Caesar's valor hath o'erthrown Antony,
But Antony's hath triumph'd on itself.
. . .
I am dying, Egypt, dying; only

I here importune death awhile, until
Of many thousand kisses the poor last
I lay upon thy lips.

He is lifted up to her tower room.

Cleopatra   And welcome, welcome! Die where thou hast lived:
Quicken with kissing: had my lips that power,
Thus would I wear them out.
                    (IV.15)

So speaks Cleopatra, and Antony with his last strength thinks only of her. He urges her to try to make her peace with Caesar—not to grieve but to remember the essential truths of his life and the honor of his death. "Now my spirit is going: I can no more," he says, and so he dies. "Unarm, Eros, the long day's task is done," he had said earlier, and slowly he had discarded one piece of his earlier "armor" after another until his spirit was wholly given to the humble love of his heart. But in Cleopatra, as is the way of woman, the final moment of transformation is sudden and complete. She is stripped of everything but essentials when she loses the beloved. She faints for a few moments; and as she revives she hears the cry of Iras, one of her women, calling her "Royal Egypt, Empress," and answers thus:

No more but e'en a woman and commanded
By such poor passion as the maid that milks
And does the meanest chores. It were for me
To throw my sceptre at the injurious gods;
To tell them that this world did equal theirs
Till they had stol'n our jewel. All's but naught;
Patience is sottish, and impatience does
Become a dog that's mad. Then is it sin
To rush into the secret house of death
Ere death dare come to us? How do you, women?
What, what! good cheer! Why, how now, Charmian!
My noble girls! Ah, women, women, look,
Our lamp is spent, it's out! Good sirs, take heart:

We'll bury him; and then, what's brave, what's noble,
Let's do it after the high Roman fashion,
And make death proud to take us. Come, away:
This case of that huge spirit now is cold.
Ah, women, women! Come; we have no friend
But resolution, and the briefest end.
      (IV.15)

Her identification with the universal image of woman, with her magical power, is past and gone forever. She is as the simplest of women in her grief, and, like Antony, she proves the truth of her love in her concern for her servants in *their* grief. She repeats again and again the word "women," as though at last she recognizes its meaning. And it is because of this that at the very end she is able to become again the Queen, claiming no power or merit but accepting in humility the royalty to which she was born, calling for her crown and her robes in which to die.

Her first words in the play's last incomparable act tells us how far from a meaningless despair are her sorrow and her resolution to die. "My desolation does begin to make a better life." Her choice of death rather than submission to Caesar and all he stands for is, in her, an affirmation of the newness of life that has arisen in her spirit.[5]

We now watch Cleopatra give a brilliant display of feminine guile as she sees through and outwits the pretended noble clemency of the triumphant Caesar. The news of Antony's death is greeted by him with tears (V.1). For a moment we see in him a spark of love, in which he recognizes his enemy as his friend and brother—though he exonerates himself as usual by comparing Antony to a disease in the body that he had to cut out in order to ensure his own survival. To the power-driven man, love is a weakness to be sternly repressed. He then announces to Cleopatra's messenger, "She soon shall know. . . how honourable and kindly we determine for her; for Caesar cannot live to be ungentle" (V.1). Whereupon he immediately sends Proculeius to assure her that Caesar intends no shame for her; he wants to make sure she will not, by killing herself, deprive him of his desire to lead her as a captive prize in his triumphal procession. After this shocking deceit he calls his followers to him, saying he will demonstrate to them how he was forced into this war and how "calm and gentle in his proceedings" he has been.

Cleopatra is not blinded for a moment. She meets the deceit with ironic words. "Tell him I am his fortune's vassal and I send him the greatness he has got. I hourly learn a doctrine of obedience" (V.2). Then, as they are about to lead her off, she tries to stab herself but is prevented, and at this point Dolabella comes and takes over the guard. This man has true sympathy for her and tells her exactly what Caesar intends.

Caesar arrives, and she puts on a most convincing act of submission and unctuous obedience—and the byplay with the treasurer Seleucas, who thinks he is betraying her to Caesar, merely shows up the far worse treachery of Caesar himself, who is sublimely unconscious of being played like a fish, until he actually says, on leaving her, "Dear queen. . . we intend so to dispose you as yourself shall give us counsel . . . . Our care and pity is so much upon you that we remain your friend" (V.2).

Caesar has been cleverly tricked into leaving her alone without a guard close to her. It would be hard to forget Maggie Smith's tone and expression as she turned to her women. "He words me, girls, he words me" (V.2) she whispers to Charmian, and sends her to hurry on that which she has already provided for as a means to die.

The Clown arrives—a simple countryman bringing the poisonous asps hidden in a basket of figs—the worm of old Nilus. Surely only Shakespeare could have achieved this marvelous scene of real humor at the very moment of high tragedy in a way that never for a moment jars us with a sense of interpolation. It is a sort of miracle; it adds a dimension of the most earthy and unsentimental reality to the intensity of feeling in the atmosphere. "The worm's an odd worm." "I wish you joy o' the worm" (V.2). Cleopatra wishes him courteously "farewell" four times before he finally stops talking and goes; immediately, without any sense of incongruity but rather with a vision of the astonishing richness of *all* life, Iras brings to Cleopatra the crown and robe for which she had called: "Go fetch my best attires. I am again for Cydnus to meet Mark Antony."

This reference to her first meeting with him, described by Enobarbus, reminds us of the spell she then cast on water and wind, as well as on the senses of man, through the power of the archetype. Antony was a mere puppet for her then. But now he is simply her man and she a woman with an aching heart, and so she may become again a Queen. I am reminded of a phrase in one of Jung's letters about his wife's last days; he speaks of "her royal death."

Being at last all woman, Cleopatra's true masculine spirit is strong in her:

> My resolution's placed, I have nothing
> Of woman in me. Now from head to foot
> I am marble-constant; now the fleeting moon
> No planet is of mine.
> . . .
> I have
> Immortal longings in me....
> . . .
> I am fire and air.
> (V.2)

Antony had spoken over and over again of his heart as he approached death; Cleopatra speaks of her newfound masculine clarity and courage. His death is by the sword that had been the instrument of his male power and aggressiveness; hers is by the poison of that cold-blooded worm hidden deep in the softness of the female being. Both sword and poison are grasped consciously now, are lifted up and transformed by sacrifice into saviors.

Most moving of all, her resolution having taken fire in action, Cleopatra becomes at last a real woman, and her final words have more simple femininity in them than would have been possible at any other time in the play: "Husband, I come. Now to that name my courage prove my title!" She kisses her women, and as she takes the asp and puts it to her breast she speaks to it gently, compassionately, as to a child: "Poor, venomous fool, be angry and dispatch." And to Charmian, "Peace, peace! Dost thou not see my baby at my breast, that sucks the nurse asleep?" "As sweet as balm, as soft as air, as gentle—O Antony!" (V.2). She dies.

Charmian's last farewell to her mistress sums up both the humanity and the royalty—the "lass" and the Queen.

So, fare thee well.
Now boast thee, death, in thy possession lies
A lass unparallel'd. Downy windows, close;
And golden Phoebus never be beheld
Of eyes again so royal!
(V.2)

Both Antony and Cleopatra have now found the "new heaven, new earth." Caesar returns, and Cleopatra in her death achieves another miracle, for even this hard, complacent realist is finally lifted out of himself into a moment of true feeling:

She looks like sleep,
As she would catch another Antony
In her strong toil of grace.
(V.2)

PART TWO

MUSINGS

ORESTEIA:
An Eye for an Eye

We look back from our peak of civilization on the blood feuds of the primitive as at something long outgrown. The impersonal retribution of the law has taken the place of private vengeance, but the instinctive demand for a death to pay for a death remains as alive as ever in the psyche, however sincerely we may consciously accept the obligation to forgive.

Before considering further the working of the revenge instinct in our own lives, we shall look at one of the great dramas of antiquity, and the three plays, called the *Oresteia*, by Aeschylus, which not only show the tragedy of human beings caught in this passion, but point forward to the possibility of its ultimate redemption. The trilogy was written in the fifth century B.C.E. at the zenith of Athenian culture and is a drama of the Greek heroic age at the end of the Trojan wars. The first two plays are concerned with the endless chain of blood for blood, but at the end of the second play, *The Libation Bearers,* the action shifts from the outer world to the inner, with the appearance of the Furies, the Eumenides. In the third play, Aeschylus imagines the beginnings of human impersonal justice, which will replace the blood feud, and then goes beyond this to another dimension and the recognition that impartial justice and reason can never be enough to end the rule of "an eye for an eye." There must also be a reconciliation of the opposites in the realm of the gods—that is, for us, in the realm of the unconscious.

The story begins long before the opening of the first play, *Agamemnon*, with the seduction of the wife of Atreus, King of Argos, by Thyestes, the king's brother. Atreus took revenge on Thyestes by inviting him to a banquet in pretended forgiveness, and then, having killed Thyestes' children, he served them up to him to eat. Only one child escaped, Aegisthus, who returned to the court of King Agamemnon (Atreus's son), nursing thoughts of revenge. Ten years before the play opens, the abduction of Helen, wife of Menelaus, Agamemnon's brother, had led to the Trojan war of revenge against Paris, Prince of Troy, a war that decimated Greece and ended with the total destruction of Troy and its population. The third cause of the tragedy in *Agamemnon* was the sacrificial killing by the king of his own daughter, Iphigenia, at the time when the Greek army was held back from sailing to Troy by unfavorable winds and the gods demanded a human sacrifice. This act had turned Clytemnestra's great love for her husband, Agamemnon, to bitter resentment and hatred. To the mother, no religious reason could redeem the horror of that killing.

Agamemnon begins in the city of Argos, where all wait for news from Troy. Clytemnestra, the queen, has governed the city for ten years with the strength and wisdom of a man, but Aegisthus has come home from exile and has become her lover, thus feeding her already passionate resentment against her absent husband with an added motive for his destruction. Aegisthus is an effeminate creature, and though he joins in the plot against Agamemnon, he keeps well out of the way when it comes to action. News comes of the fall of Troy, and the king returns in triumph, but it is an empty one in spite of big words. The flower of Greek manhood is dead, there are very few survivors, and we feel the full horror of the enormous price in human life and misery that has been paid for the paltry end of revenging one man for the loss of his wife. Agamemnon brings with him Cassandra, the captive Trojan princess, who is his mistress (allowed to Greek warriors in war). Here is yet more fuel for the fire of Clytemnestra's resentment, and she is bitterly jealous, for she both loves and hates Agamemnon and will kill the thing she loves. He has betrayed her as mother; now he betrays her as wife. She meets Agamemnon with simulated joy and flattery. He asserts his freedom from undue pride but really swallows her flattery, and the symbol of this is his walking on the robe she has spread on the ground for him, and with which she is about to trap him. He enters the house, and while he is in the bath, she entangles him in the robe and stabs him to death.

The audience waits outside with the chorus. Clytemnestra emerges. She dominates the play, and one is somehow compelled to respect her as she takes full responsibility for her deed. Like all avengers, she claims to have carried out a *cleansing.* "Now all is paid and men may live in peace," is their cry. Orestes is to make the same claim in the next play. But the bloodshed in revenge begets another revenge and so on without end.

In *The Libation Bearers*, the second play, Orestes, son of Agamemnon and Clytemnestra, who had been sent away from home as a child before his father's return, has grown up and returns to avenge his father. He meets Electra, his sister, at Agamemnon's tomb, to which she has brought libations. Together they plot to kill Aegisthus and Clytemnestra, their mother. They have to whip up their courage for this worst of all crimes, telling themselves it is a cleansing of evil, casting themselves into a fury of self-pity and finally putting the blame on the gods; for the Delphic oracle of Apollo has ordered Orestes to kill his mother. Face to face with her, however, he still hesitates. The love between them almost defeats the mutual hatred and fear, but we know that she would have killed him out of fear and in spite of love, just as he will kill her out of hatred. The memory of the oracle tips the scale and he stabs her. "Now," he cries, "I will take my rightful kingdom and rule in peace; all is cleansed." The triumph is shortlived. Remorse invades him and immediately the Furies appear, the avenging spirits of the Mother, and he runs from his kingdom to wander, homeless and terrified. Revenge has passed from the outer to the inner world.

In *The Eumenides*, the third play, the issue is first between man and the gods and finally between Apollo, the god of reason, and the dark instincts of the unconscious. Orestes' personal murder of his mother may be seen as a symbol of the murder by man's growing consciousness of his primitive identity with the unconscious world of the instincts. The Furies were not activated by any of the other murders—by the husband's murder, the horrors of the war, not even by the horrible killing of the children. Matricide is in another category, the unforgivable crime in the eyes of nature.

The Furies were those terrible goddesses whose hair was writhing snakes, but most strangely their name, the *Eumenides*, actually means the Kindly Ones. It is one of the great paradoxes. Revenge is the chief characteristic of the witch, the rejected and repressed side of the feminine image, and we may notice that every one of the crimes in this story is set in motion by a betrayal of woman, of the true feeling values. The seduction of Atreus's wife and of Helen, Agamemnon's unnatural sacrifice, Clytemnestra's infidelity, all culminate in the murder of the mother, the symbol of the rejection of great Mother Nature herself.

Athens in Aeschylus's day was in fact moving into a dangerous split from the feminine values of nature, a split that in our day has reached terrifying proportions, and the wisdom of Aeschylus is more than ever valid for us. In *The Eumenides* he is little concerned with Orestes' personal story and sees the issue in depth as a problem of all humankind. The gods are the protagonists—there is no hope at all for a solution unless a mediator can be found; Apollo and the Furies, reason and instinct, would forever remain implacable enemies. In the play this mediating function is personified in Pallas Athene, who was for the ancient Greeks the symbol of masculine courage and understanding united to feminine feeling and instinctive wisdom.

Orestes, seeking sanctuary at Delphi with Apollo (who can at least send the Furies to sleep when he is around but can never drive them away), is sent by him to Athens to appeal to Athene. Reason in the Greeks was still in touch with the unconscious (Apollo spoke through the Sybil at Delphi) and therefore knew the need for a mediator, whereas nowadays reason all too often becomes rationality, which simply dismisses feminine values as nonsense. The Furies follow Orestes, breathing threats, and Athene's first response to her supplicant is to call a jury of citizens to try Orestes. Law is to be substituted for blood feud. Orestes admits his crime and pleads justification by his mother's wickedness and Apollo's explicit order. The Furies say that nothing whatever can excuse matricide. The jury is equally divided, and Athene gives her casting vote for Orestes. Civilized objective thinking can stop the chain of revenge on the outer level, but Athene very well knows that this can also result in driving the conflict underground where it will do far greater damage. Therefore, while her masculine judgment speaks for Orestes, she knows in her feminine wisdom that the Furies are also right and must be accepted. Apollo had rejected them utterly, identifying them with evil and everything regressive, emotional, uncivilized. It is as though Athene penetrates to the inner meaning of the Delphic oracle. It is true that man must free himself from the devouring mother who murders the values of consciousness, but not by means of another murder. Real freedom can only come through accepting inwardly the furies of instinct without loss of conscious values, thus redeeming them.

The Furies now utter horrible threats. They will poison the crops of the Athenians, bring disease and misery on all. Athene speaks to them gently, with persuasion, with respect. She knows that, if civilized justice and reason become identified with the Apollonian values as the only good, the destructiveness of the ancient mother goddesses will erupt in untold evil for mankind. The "murder" of the instinctive and the irrational by civilized consciousness will result in the final poisoning of everything, in outbursts of fury and killing on a collective scale infinitely worse than the personal blood feud, as we, today, so very well know. Athene, therefore, on behalf of her citizens, offers the raging goddesses acceptance and love. Aeschylus calls them "the ancient children," for they have the ruthlessness but also the spontaneous vitality of the child, and this a man rejects to his own undoing. If they in turn will accept this offer, absorb their anger in the nourishing aspect of their nature, then men will worship them in love instead of fear. They will preside over fertility in all its forms, the true function of the mother image. Instead of wandering in the dark, outcast, preying on the unconscious of man, they will have a place in every home, bringing richness to the crops, happiness in marriage, good fortune in childbirth—nourishment, in fact, to all the life-giving forces of nature. At first they will not believe Athene, but finally they are won over, as they always are when a man will face their terrifying power with the respect and acceptance of Athene. They exchange their snake headgear for green olive branches, and the citizens lead them to their new home with a beautiful song, which ends the play.

So far does Aeschylus take us. He shows what must happen if civilization is to survive, and that only the "Athene" within us can effect the reconciliation. But how are we as individuals to bring to birth this reconciling symbol? Orestes in the play makes a quick journey to the city of Athene, which is passed over in silence. For each of us, however, who has identified with the Apollonian point of view, it is a long and difficult road, demanding a searching honesty and courage. The first step is surely to rid ourselves of the idea that we have outgrown the law of "an eye for an eye." We have to expose the delusion that, to forgive our enemies in accord with Christian ethic, it is only necessary to behave in an outwardly civilized manner, without bothering about what our repressed fury is doing. Every time we are hurt or angry or resentful toward a person, a circumstance, or even a material thing, a desire to inflict an equivalent hurt is born, however unconscious we may be of it. We have suffered a little death and the desire to kill follows, for it is the nature of the psyche to seek always a restored balance. Demands refused, efforts frustrated, humiliations real or imagined, all breed the desire to effect a small "cleansing," as Clytemnestra did in her rage. But the new injury implies another, and so on without end. The fact that the injury is unseen merely increases its force. Husband, wife, children, or friends can be driven by this hidden revenge into all manner of darkness.

The Christian answer is to turn the other cheek, but if we stop there we miss the whole meaning of Christ's message and only fall more deeply into this deadly menace of peace by repression. If we turn the other cheek, we are not thereby released from the law of the psyche, which demands a death for a death. It is better to have a blazing row than imagine this. The true "turning of the other cheek" is the full recognition of this law together with the willingness to accept the necessary death *within ourselves,* which is the only way to prevent its infliction on someone else, whether consciously or unconsciously. This is the whole answer as we see it in the life and death of Christ. "One jot or one tittle," he said, "shall in no wise pass from the law until all be fulfilled." This law of a death for a death is to be fulfilled by the injured individual himself, by one's recognition of the fact that the other one's guilt is also in a deep sense one's own, and by one's consent, in the midst of perhaps legitimate resentment, to pay the price, to die a little to the demand for justification and immunity. We may imagine for a moment how Clytemnestra might have seen Agamemnon as part of herself, not repressing her desire to kill him, but recognizing it on a deeper level as the desire to wipe out her *own* guilt, which is the root of all revenge. Actually the things she hated him for were precisely her own sins. She, too, had a lover; she too "murdered" inwardly her son and her daughter and was caught in an overweening pride. Jung has written of capital punishment that it is an assuaging, on a collective level, of each person's unconscious guilt for his own will to murder. The only end to this chain of blood for blood is in the individual's willingness to pay with his own blood for every injury he sustains. This and this only is the way to the discovery of the Athene within, the power that can meet the furies of the unconscious with love, and so discover in the heart of the fury itself the great nourishing, life-giving power of the all-forgiving Mother within.

THE STRANGER WITHIN

The *American Heritage Dictionary* tells us that the Indo-European root of the words "host," "hospice," "hospitality," and "hospital" is *ghosti*; it is, surprisingly, also the root of the word "guest." Moreover, in the Indo-European Appendix the meaning of this root includes another word: ghosti meant "stranger" as well as "guest" and "host," properly, "someone with whom one has reciprocal duties of hospitality." There follows yet another meaning: from this root word also came the English "hostile," via the second meaning of "host" as a multitude—often of enemies. This, again, is connected to the fear of the unknown, which leads to the frequent projection of suspicion and hostility onto anything or any person that is strange to us.

Russell Lockhart, in his splendid book *Words As Eggs*,[1] has said that behind every word that we use—for the most part so casually—there lies a story to be found, if we are willing to attend to its inner meaning. There is a level on which the essential story will be the same for all seekers, but also a level where it will be unique for every one of us. As the pattern of every snowflake is unique, so also are the stories that nourish every single human life.

Most men and women who seek wholeness, or in Dante's words, "the love that moves the sun and the other stars," will easily recognize consciously the outer duties of hospitality whether as host or guest. (I hope that throughout this bit of writing readers will know that in this context "host" includes both genders, so that they will not accuse me of ignoring the hostess! The word "host" transcends gender.) However, the degree to which we live the beauty and courtesy of the exchanges between hosts and guests, particularly when we are strangers to one another, will surely depend on our attitude to those inner images that are either the guiding truths of our lives, or, especially while they remain wholly unconscious or repressed, the controlling addictions or hidden goals of the psyche.

Imagination in its fundamental meaning, as defined by Shakespeare or Blake, and known to all great creative artists, is the making and the responding to images of all kinds in the outer and inner worlds. We don't have to be great artists to do this; every one of us has the ability to respond by at least beginning to say "yes" or "no" to the strangers who knock on the doors of our souls—even if our clear and honest response is "I am too weak to confront this threatening hostile stranger. I am as I am." That too may be the saving humility that admits the divine and transforming guest; but to shut one's ears and eyes and ignore the knocking within delivers the ego over to possession by the demand for security or power, from which is born anger, violence, and hardness of heart. How easy it then is to be blind to the needs of those we meet—especially if they are personalities who irritate or bore us—because only a truly imaginative response can keep us aware of the effect on the other of an insensitive lack of warmth in our welcome.

I have had considerable experience with the messages that come to us through dreams. The voice of the dream will either warn of dangers in our attitudes to the journey of life or else give us courage as it points the way to new awareness. Thus we are enabled to take up the responsibilities of joy and so to find the kind of imaginative exchange that heals and unites. A very common theme in the dreams of someone who is unconsciously resisting a new awareness of such a responsibility, evading some hidden creative ability in him- or herself, is that of a burglar or terrifying unknown person, or even a monster, who has broken into the house or is trying to get in to steal or perhaps to kill. The dreamer is often terrified and trying desperately in the dream to call the police, or find some means of evasion or escape from the intruder and so banish the threat to his or her inner security. Sometimes, as Marie-Louise von Franz has written in one of her fairy tale books, it is *necessary* for the one threatened to run away. Much discrimination is needed to recognize these occasions.

However, more often when the stranger takes this form, it becomes clear that the unknown or as yet rejected new attitude has turned dangerously negative and threatening, determined to make itself felt. If the dreamer is able in imagination to turn the dream into a story, into which he or she actively enters—opening the door perhaps and confronting the intruder, asking what his need is, inviting him in as one would a guest—then a conversation may ensue, a recognition, a lessening of fear. Gradually, if the dreamer truly attends and does not just forget it all after a day or two, the changed attitude begins to alter behavior, and even leads to a long-resisted major change in the way of life. Thus do one's personal images bring to mind the great stories in the myths.

We remember that among so-called primitive people a stranger who came to the door of a tent or home, seeking shelter and food, was to be welcomed as an honored guest, especially because so easily he might be a god in disguise, even if he could also be a disguised enemy. We may also remember those saints or sages in all the great religious traditions who would invite an obvious thief to take any of their possessions and make no effort to oppose him—and, more delightful still, the many hermits, and indeed the great naturalists of our time, who realize they are the guests, as it were, of the wild animals into whose land they intrude, and who treat the creatures with respect and love and so are not threatened by them. As an example, I saw a program on PBS recently in which the white wolf mother of a pack on Ellesmere Island (in the Arctic, north of Canada) positively invited the man (whose name, I regret, I have forgotten) who had been living there in a tent for many months to enter her den and see her new cubs. The exchanges of true hospitality were between them.

It is sad when we compare this to the almost universal collective behavior of civilized man as he explored new lands in search of power or wealth. Any thought of being a guest of those races who had lived there for thousands of years came only to the very few, and it may be that the worst damage of all was done by those who, with excellent intentions, tried to "rescue" their hosts from their ancient traditions and ways of life. Nevertheless, as always, there are the shining stories of great individuals—travelers and explorers—in whom the respect and courtesy of the true guest and host stand out and the patient interest of "reciprocal hospitality" has brought about a final trust even after centuries of hostility. To mention one example among many in our own time, Laurens van der Post's books about the Bushmen—the first men of Africa—are a constant joy, recreating in the reader glimpses of the power and beauty of this latent spirit of hospitality in all the true meanings of our inner and outer lives.[2]

More than fifty years ago, I myself had the great good fortune to experience with my husband the extraordinarily gracious and spontaneous hospitality of a small group of Bedouin in the desert beyond Aman in Jordan when our car broke down. It was near sunset, and we were welcomed into the young sheik's tent, given water to wash with, fed with specially prepared food, and entertained in every way they could devise without a shared language, as we waited for a mechanic, fetched by one of their young men who was sent on foot to the nearest village. Night fell and the stars shone out in the clear desert air while camels sat around resting. We were even offered a night's shelter. The experience left a living memory of the essential courtesy to the stranger in a strange land—a welcome with no hidden demand for any return, no questions asked—a free giving and taking of the simplest kind.

Perhaps it is because of this memory that the great hospitality story in our own tradition—one that stands out for me as of a particular power when we turn to the very difficult task of creating this kind of simple guest and host exchange with the unknown aspects of ourselves—is the story of the coming of three men to Abraham in his old age (he was 99) as he sat at the entrance to his desert tent. After he had welcomed them and brought them water and food, the strangers asked him where his wife Sarah was, and then told them both that she would conceive and bear a child. But Sarah laughed to herself, thinking them foolish, knowing that it was impossible at her age. And the guest (who had become one, it seems, instead of three, and was indeed Yahweh himself) asked, "Why did Sarah laugh... is anything too wonderful for Yahweh?" "I did not laugh," said Sarah, lying because she was afraid. But he replied, "Oh, yes, you did laugh."

However, "Yahweh dealt kindly with Sarah... and did what he had promised her"—in spite of her somewhat contemptuous laughter at such nonsense. So Sarah conceived and bore a son to Abraham in his old age. And then comes the altogether delightful ending to the story. Sarah said, "God has given me cause to laugh; all those who hear of it will laugh with me."[3] From the laughter of rejection she has brought to birth the child and found the laughter at the heart of life in which all with ears to hear may join.

So it can be with all those strange and seemingly hostile or meaningless images that knock at our doors, either in dreams or in irrational moods, in emotions or cravings, in unnoticed use of words or habits of movement, both physical and psychic. If we dream, we may experience all these habits and unconscious patterns already personified (though of course one needs a guide). If that is not our way, we can allow our imagination to do the same for them, and we may recognize them perhaps in our projections onto others, and then we may treat them all as the strange and unknown guests within who have been wandering without food or water—that is, starving and withering from lack of acceptance, growing hostile and angry, and so shaking us awake. Then indeed we discover that they bring us a message from the Spirit within, from the Self, the God of innumerable names, the I Am That I Am. The message is a birth in us—even a rebirth of the inner child—a newness of life and laughter, no matter how impossible that may seem, as the stranger brought the child to Sarah in her old age.

In all the stories the emphasis is on food and drink—always symbols of the kind of attention and concern that is the essence of hospitality. The guest is to be offered nourishment on every level—nourishment of the kind we all need, the best we can offer, and emphatically not our own concept of what is "good for" the other, including the other within. It is easy to forget that only to the extent that we listen and attend to these figures who express our own weaknesses and potential strengths have we any hope of recognizing, in all those we meet in the outer world, either their needs as guests to be honored by us whether we like them or not, or their dues as hosts as they offer to us their acceptance and trust. We may find it hard to personify these unconscious denizens of the psyche; but mere "good" resolutions never change anything fundamentally. Shakespeare tells us that "the lunatic, the lover and the poet are of imagination all compact."[4] Within us these strangers bring the divine guest who transforms us, often through simple and unnoticed actions. That doesn't mean that we must necessarily write poetry or paint pictures, but simply allow the "poet" within us to give "a local habitation and a name"[5] to our strange inner guests. When the reciprocal rules of hospitality have become a spontaneous and joyful reality in the soul, then the divine spark will live between the individual and the other in all her or his meetings with every form of life.

Although it is so well known, I want to end with some brief quotations from that story, beloved among all the Greek myths—the tale of Baucis and Philemon, as told by the Roman poet Ovid in his *Metamorphoses,* and translated by the American poet Rolfe Humphries.[6] Humphries' translation conveys to us in our own language, with sheer delight, the spontaneous essence of true hospitality, as Ovid describes the actions of two souls who have grown into the simplicity of that love which no abstract words can describe—the love in which mind and heart and instinct are at one in the web of life, in time and in eternity.

Ovid describes how Jupiter and Mercury, disguised as mortals, traveled the earth looking for rest.

> They found a thousand houses
> Shut in their face. But one at last received them
> A humble cottage thatched with straw and reeds,
> A good old woman, Baucis, and her husband
> A good old man, Philemon, used to live there.
> They had married young, they had grown old together
> In the same cottage; they were very poor,
> But faced their poverty with cheerful spirit
> And made its burden light by not complaining.
> It would do you little good to ask for servants
> Or masters in that household, for the couple
> Were all the house; both gave and followed orders.
> So, when the gods came to this little cottage,
> Ducking their heads to enter, the old man
> Pulled out a rustic bench for them to sit on,
> And Baucis spread a homespun cover for it.

There is no male superiority in this house! Ovid goes on to describe the kindling of the fire, blown by Baucis, who hadn't much breath to spare in her old age; the cooking in a copper kettle of the cabbage brought in from their well-watered garden by Philemon, and a chunk of their precious side of bacon. And they made conversation

> To keep the time from being too long. . . .
> Baucis, her skirts tucked up, was setting the table
> With trembling hands. One table leg was wobbly,
> A piece of shell fixed that.

The food is described, cottage cheese and eggs. The earthenware and the wine "of no particular vintage

> and apples in wide baskets—
> Remember how apples smell?—and purple grapes
> Fresh from the vines, and a white honeycomb
> As centerpiece, and all around the table

Shone kindly faces, nothing mean or poor
Or skimpy in good will.

Then they noticed that the mixing bowl kept filling up all by itself.
That scared them, and they thought anxiously that their food wasn't
good enough for such guests and wanted to kill their precious goose,
who was a sort of watchdog for them. But the goose ran to the gods and
they revealed themselves, preventing the killing, and took the old cou-
ple up the mountain, from which they saw that the houses in the valley
whose doors had been closed to the strangers were now flooded with
water—all except their cottage. "And while they wondered they wept a
little for their neighbors' troubles." Their cottage was now turning into
a temple, and Jupiter asked them what they would like for themselves.

And they hesitated,
Asked, could we talk it over just a little?
And talked together apart.

Then Philemon spoke for both and asked that they might be priests
having care of the temple and that they might die in the same hour.

And one day as they stood before the temple
Both very old, talking the old days over
Each saw the other put forth leaves, Philemon
Watched Baucis changing, Baucis watched Philemon
And as the foliage spread, they still had time
To say "Farewell, my dear. . . . "
The peasants in that district still show the stranger
The two trees close together, and the union
Of oak and linden in one.

The beautiful ending of this story is a simple, natural image of the
hierosgamos, the final unity, the marriage of opposites in which duality
is transcended yet each partner remains unique—the oak and the linden
remain themselves as their roots and branches intertwine in a single tree
of life. The two old people had become hosts and guests to each other
in their daily lives, and so to all life—to the gods and to all the unknown

who came to their temple to honor and worship the divine images in
their own hearts.

Ovid ends his poem by telling how he himself had seen this tree—
one and yet still two—and brought a garland and said a verse:

> The gods look after good people still, and cherishers are
> cherished.

JACOB AND ESAU

In the mythology of the Judeo-Christian tradition, the theme of the two brothers at enmity begins after the Fall with Cain and Abel, continues with Isaac and Ishmael, and culminates in the much more complicated story of Jacob and Esau, who were the first twins. It is because of the image of twinship that their story, particularly its ending, is of such profound relevance in this our century, when the separation between twins—an image of the two sides, as it were, of one man or woman, and of the twinship of nature and spirit on every level—has become the most terrible danger, threatening the survival of all life on this planet.

Jacob and Esau fought in Rebecca's womb, but it was Esau who was the natural first-born—Jacob had to hold onto his heel in order to arrive almost as one child with him. Esau remained the first-born, with Jacob at his heels, and their oneness, their equality of value in the sight of God and in the life of the earth cannot be doubted. Jacob was white-skinned and smooth, a man of "the tents," his mother's favorite, cunning of mind and sensitive, fearful even, but also with a love of beauty, we may imagine, already capable of discrimination. Esau was called Edom, which means "the red one." He was hairy and red, strong of body, and lived in the impulse of the moment. Red is the color of fire and is symbolic both of the flame of the spirit—of purification, of light and heat—and equally of the fire that destroys and consumes. Red represents the impulsive, emotional, instinctive nature which, if it is in control, can smother all approaches to meaning and so become evil. If, on the other hand, this nature is repressed and denied, it will leave the conscious personality dry and unreal and finally completely possessed by greed for power. Therefore Set in Egypt, the dark brother of Osiris, was also called the red one, and Mephistopheles by tradition always wore red. But without the Promethean theft of fire there could have been no human kind, no way to the conscious knowledge of dark and light, no carrier of the imaginative spark that can find the fire that transcends the split and opens the door to that which is beyond all opposites.

I have written elsewhere of Jacob's early story[1]—of his stealing of "the blessing" of his birthright through the urging of his mother, of

Rebecca's wisdom and acceptance of her guilt and of her separation from Jacob. Jacob also pays for the stolen blessing by remaining separate from his twin. He serves seven long years of waiting to marry Rachel, the true partner of his spirit, who bears his beloved son Joseph. Through the deceit of Laban, Jacob is also bound for life to Leah. Jacob's story continues when he returns to his own country accompanied by Rachel and Leah, their offspring, and all his collected riches and flocks. When he learns that Esau is coming to meet him with four hundred men, he is terrified, remembering his sin against his brother. Knowing he must face the fear, he sends everyone away in order to spend the night alone, wrestling with his darkness.

The account of that night is unforgettable: "And there wrestled a man with him until the breaking of the day" (Gen. 32). It is a moving story of a man's struggle with the unknown in himself, expressing absolute determination to know the stranger, to learn his name. He realizes that the seeming enemy is the one who can bless him individually and from within, not just ritually and from without as in his early unconscious days. Wounded in the thigh, exhausted from long hours of effort, he says, "I will not let thee go, except thou bless me." The moment of transformation comes with the speaking of his new name, "Israel."

Then, when Jacob asks the vital question, "Tell me, I pray thee, thy name," he receives full blessing. The hidden name cannot be humanly spoken, but, as in other myths, though the answer may not be given, the issue hangs on asking the right question at the right time. Jacob now knows that in this long struggle of love he has "seen God face to face," and his life is preserved.

Now Jacob is ready to meet his human brother. No more is said of his fear (except that he sends gifts ahead as a protection!). There is an indication in the text of how deeply Jacob's previous struggle was connected with his twin when he repeats at the meeting with Esau almost the exact words he had used after the stranger blessed him. "I have seen thy face," he says to Esau, "as though I had seen the face of God" (Gen. 33:10). He has not confused the levels of experience—this is evident in the words "as though"—but it seems that the experience of the night before has made possible this seeing of the divine in the face of his opposite, the long-estranged red brother.

Now the simple and affectionate Esau thinks they can settle down together, living "next door," so to speak—but Jacob knows it is too soon for that. Again he retreats to trickery, saying he is forced to travel more slowly than his brother, and when Esau trustingly sets off, Jacob takes another direction. Instead of keeping in touch with Esau, he begins the long process of putting him entirely out of his mind, and Esau is not mentioned again in the story. Thus the seed of the distant future was sown so that in the subsequent centuries the growing contempt and rejection of natural man and of his so-called primitive religions and way of life even brought attempts to eliminate whole populations. Then, the growth of consciousness brought our age of technology, so often devastatingly misused.

Collectively, we have lost the wonder of stones and soil, of animals and birds, and we have lost the spontaneous voices of dream and vision, without which the people perish. But there are also individuals who recognize the natural "red one" within and without, feeling the same fire that the hubris of the intellect had turned into greed for power. There is a new wish to return to the gifts of our mother the earth. We may, as C. G. Jung said, come to a global, cosmic rebirth in this darkest time, if enough individuals will wrestle with the unknown God and ask his name—and see in our rejected twin the face of God.

The Laughter at
the Heart of Things

I t is impossible to define that which we call "a sense of humor"; and yet perhaps by playing around it in imagination we may bring to light a little of the wonder, the mystery, of that divine and human gift. Barbara Hannah wrote of C. G. Jung that he often used to quote Schopenhauer, who said, "A sense of humor is the only divine quality of man."[1]

Humor itself is a word of many meanings. In the Middle Ages and through the Renaissance it meant, among other things, one of the four principal body fluids that determine human dispositions and health (sanguine, phlegmatic, choleric, melancholic); and in physiology it still means "any clear or hyaline [transparent] body fluid such as blood, lymph, or bile." Some other definitions in the *American Heritage Dictionary* are: "the quality of being laughable or comical," "a state of mind, mood, spirit," "a sudden unanticipated whim." The root of the word is the Latin *umor* meaning "liquid, fluid." Humor, therefore, on all levels is something that flows, resembling water itself, and symbolizes the movement of unconscious forces gradually evolving into basic characteristics of the individual human being, which express themselves in the body, in moods and emotional reactions, in qualities of feeling, of mind, and of spirit.

The *sense* of humor, however, has a far more elusive meaning. The *American Heritage Dictionary,* in defining "sense," after mentioning the five senses we share with the animals, continues, "Intuitive or acquired perception or ability to estimate (a sense of timing). A capacity to appreciate or understand (a sense of humor). Recognition or perception either through the senses or the intellect (a sense of guilt)."

Our humors, therefore, are unconscious drives or reactions, but without consciousness there can be no *sense* of humor at all, however much we may enjoy jokes and absurdities. It is especially interesting that the kind of sense or perception defined as a capacity "to appreciate and understand" is illustrated by a reference to "a sense of humor." The other definitions speak of the senses or the intellect or intuition; only "appreciation and understanding" are words that bring the heart into the matter. This may be a hint to us that the wisdom and compassion of the understanding heart are indeed the core of the laughter that is born from the mature sense of humor.

Most people do not think about the essential difference between a sense of humor and mere reactions to any kind of comical situation. All such things *may* induce laughter whether we have a real sense of humor or not. But the quality of the laughter is very different in those who "appreciate and understand." Those without that kind of perception do not penetrate to the "laughter at the heart of things" of which T. S. Eliot spoke in his introduction to Charles Williams' last novel, *All Hallows' Eve*.[2] Eliot writes of Williams' stories that even for people who never read a novel more than once they are good entertainment, and continues:

> I believe that is how Williams himself would like them to be read, the first time; for he was a gay and simple man with a keen sense of entertainment and drollery. The deeper things are there just because they belonged to the world he lived in and he could not have kept them out. For the reader who can appreciate them there are terrors in the pit of darkness into which he can make us look; but in the end, we are brought nearer to what another modern explorer of the darkness has called "the laughter at the heart of things."

Eliot does not name that other modern explorer, but his words express a fundamental truth about those people of whom we can truly say that they possess and communicate a sense of humor. Unless a man or woman has experienced the darkness of the soul he or she can know nothing of that transforming laughter without which no hint of the ultimate unity of the opposites can be faintly intuited.

In all the greatest poets, mystics, and storytellers this sense of humor shines, even when not expressed recognizably in words and images that inspire laughter—even when they are conveying tragedy and sorrow and the darkest experiences of human life. For a very little consideration will show us clearly that the sense of humor is always born of a *sense of proportion,* both in the inner world and in the outer. The sense or perception of proportion means the capacity to discriminate and respond to ("understand and appreciate") the relationship of the parts of anything to the whole. "Proportion is the desirable, correct, or perfect relationship of parts within a whole" (*American Heritage Dictionary*). If we come to the point of retaining a sense of proportion in the midst of all the smallest as well as in the most profound of human emotions, we shall also discover that at the center of every experience is that laughter of God which Meister Eckhart, among many, affirmed with such delight.

There are so many kinds of laughter, and it often conceals a bitterly destructive rejection or contempt. When we yield to that we are cut off altogether from the sense of humor that always strengthens the compassion in which all our pains and joys become whole. Hurt vanity (our own or another's), personal resentments or anger, humiliations or demands for some change in another—the antics of our alternately inflated or deflated egos—can be accepted with pain and known also as occasions for the laughter that heals. In this laughter we recognize them at once as a temporary loss of "relationship to the whole," to the center that is everywhere. Charles Williams has a wonderful phrase (I think it occurs in one of his poems): he speaks of "the excellent absurdity" of any achievement of leadership or power. A man's fate, the meaning of his individual life on earth, is simply to live fully his own particular small part in the pattern of the whole, whether seemingly great or seemingly most ordinary, retaining always that blessed sense of humor about its importance to ourselves or to others with at least the "intention of Joy" (Williams' phrase) even in the midst of emotional pain.

Humility is without question closely related to the sense of humor. The one surely cannot exist without the other. Once more I quote from T. S. Eliot writing about Charles Williams in the introduction to *All Hallows' Eve* mentioned above. The essence of what he says could certainly have been written about any one of those explorers of darkness whose lives and words bring the sound of that laughter to the listening ear.

> He appeared completely at ease in surroundings... which had intimidated many; and at the same time was modest and unassuming to the point of humility: that unconscious humility, one discovered later, was in him a natural quality, one he possessed to a degree which made one, in time, feel very humble oneself in his presence.[3]

> Williams never appeared to wish to impress, still less to dominate; he talked with a kind of modest and retiring loquacity. His conversation was so easy and informal, taking its start from the ordinary

trifles and humorous small talk of the occasion; it passed so quickly and naturally between the commonplace and the original, between the superficial and the profound. . . appreciation of its value came the more slowly because of his quickness to defer and to listen.[4]

Eliot is expressing here the identity of a sense of humor with the sense of *proportion* and the humility that this engenders.

C. G. Jung was another, and one of the greatest, of the explorers of the darkness in this century. He consciously entered the "pit of darkness" in the unconscious and, evading no fact of evil and its horrors, found also "the laughter at the heart of things." Many who knew him well have testified to the quality of his sense of humor and of his laughter, and Laurens van der Post, in his biography of Jung,[5] wrote a beautiful tribute. He compared Jung's laughter to the laughter of the Bushmen of Africa, thus linking it to the instinctive gaiety of the natural man, of the child, who has not lost his original unity with nature. (Williams also spoke of this gaiety in *The Greater Trumps* as an intrinsic attribute of natural intelligence.) But this natural laughter must surely die when the growth of ego-consciousness plunges the individual into the terrible conflicts of the human condition before it is given back at the birth of joy. In between lies "the ethical phase—endurance and action," as Jung once expressed it in a letter.[6] This is the phase of exploration, of purgatorial choices and confrontations, in which we learn to behave "as if" we knew joy without ever disguising to ourselves the actual state of our emotions: then, sooner or later, the true gift of that laughter will come to us, when we least expect it, through the response to life which is a sense of humor—the realization of proportion.

The original gaiety of the natural man had certainly undergone a night-sea-journey in Jung as it must in everyone seeking conscious wholeness. The adolescent ego must go through the struggle to establish its identity as separate from parents and environment—a process often prolonged throughout a lifetime. In this inner struggle we are frequently caught in a sense of the earth-shaking importance of our achievements, which is a normal phase in the young. But the individual may tragically remain obsessed into adult years with his or her superiority or inferiority as the case may be. Nothing more quickly kills the ability to laugh at oneself which is the sure mark of a sense of humor. We are then left with the sterile moralities of convention, a kind of solemn and possessive pursuit of "spirituality" from which the wind that "bloweth where it listeth" and its laughter are entirely absent. The opposites of these moralities—senseless rebellion, violence, license, greed, and corruption—can never be controlled by such attitudes. Only the far more difficult search for the ethics of individual freedom and joy can avail in our predicament.

A sense of humor is in fact the royal road to this freedom and this joy. One who has it is always ready to laugh at all the pretensions of the ego in him- or herself or in another. This differentiates it at once from intellectual wit and superficial joking and, still more obviously, from the forced cheerfulness of some who are determined always to do "good," to improve the ego and the world.

Without this kind of humor no one can experience the laughter of the reborn Child within, for it brings with it a recognition of the fundamental validity of the "other," of object and subject as one. People who lack this perception may laugh in the same situations, but there is a subtle difference in their laughter, for it does not spring from the heart and the belly; at its worst it often contains hidden barbs directed at another, since it is a protective armor for a frightened ego. We all laugh at the foibles of those around us, but those with a sense of humor do not laugh *at* a person; there is simply a feeling of delight in the ridiculous wherever it is manifest, and such laughter does not condemn the other or oneself but simply enjoys the sudden recognition of the loss of proportion in all our human conflicts and contradictions. It is a healing, not a destructive thing—a delight in life, in its comedies and tragedies, its seriousness and absurdities—the "excellent absurdities" that Williams loved.

"There are many ways of laughing," wrote van der Post of Jung's laugh, "but the greatest is that which comes from the joy of seeing disproportion restored to proportion. His laughter was delight, sheer and uncompromising, in the triumph of the significance of the small over the unreality of excess and disproportion in the established great, and so a pure rejoicing in another enlargement, however minute, of the dominion of proportion."[7] Let us repeat the definition of this powerful word, "the perfect relationship of the parts to the whole."

It is a sad, even a dangerous loss to Christianity that the Gospels and so many of their interpreters never convey the sense of humor that Jesus must certainly have manifested in his life, and we are told nothing of the laughter that must have been so often heard from him and with him. But if one listens imaginatively to some of the stories and sayings it is clearly to be heard. After his ultimate exploration of darkness and the "descent into Hell" it ripples and flows with such joy in the resurrection stories that the absence of specific references to it cannot hide it. When in later centuries the lives of saints and sages have been described, how often their laughter lifts our hearts. St. Teresa's autobiography, for instance, dances with it.

There is, in fact, no real "spirituality" (a much misunderstood term in these days) without the laughter that the sense of humor brings. It is not to be confused with frivolity, and it cannot exist in anyone who is not a serious person able to explore the darkness and suffering in life. The lack of this quality in the soul may also reveal itself among those who seek to lighten the solemnity of their religious beliefs by *mixing* the funny and the serious, making jokes, either silly or embarrassing, *about* the deep realities. The sense of humor, the laughter of the Self, never *mixes* things in that way, thus destroying both the serious and the gay. It simply begets in men and women a true perception of all the suffering and the joy, the tears and laughter, the seriousness and the fun, inherent in our experience. When all these opposites are clearly discriminated they may then be known as one in the unity of the laughter and the tragic darkness of being.

In the diaries of Etty Hillesum,[8] this young Dutch Jewish woman, writing during the occupation of Holland by the Nazis, told of the horrible suffering of those, including herself, waiting in a camp for transportation to Auschwitz (where she was to die). Her compassion, not only for the victims but for the Germans who inflicted the suffering, shines out from the book, but most moving of all are her words, in the midst of the horrors, about her experience of the deepest and most radiant inner joy she had ever known. She tells how she realized what a very little thing all this misery was in the glorious wholeness of the universe. Her joy was the dawning of the sense of proportion, the relationship of every part, however dark, to the whole.

As we wonder how we could possibly have endured such a fate, we are nevertheless inspired by these great ones urgently to seek in our everyday lives a fuller realization of this joy, this laughter. The humdrum tasks, the endless repetitions of the daily round, are often much more difficult to recognize as occasions for this kind of vivid living in the moment than are the more dramatic events of our lives. We hurry through the so-called boring things in order to attend to that which we deem more important and interesting. Perhaps the final freedom will be a recognition that every thing in every moment is *"essential"* and that nothing at all is *"important"*!

The first step on this way is to learn all over again that natural gift of the small child—the gift of play—which is so conspicuously absent from our society. The natural gaiety and laughter of the child within us is lost in exact proportion to the loss of our ability to play; and it is fascinating to remember the many contexts in which that word is used. We use it unconsciously without any thought of its fundamental meaning and therefore the word so often loses its connection with that natural joy. Every kind of dramatic performance is called a play, and all actors are players, as are all musicians, and all ball- and game-players. Tragedy, comedy, farce, and all kinds of music—Bach, plainsong, jazz, or rock and roll—are brought to us by players among whom there are those who appreciate and understand the nature of play and so convey the joy of it to their audiences whether through their "playing" of dark truths or light. But there are so many who have no perception of the meaning of play and whose striving motives are to acquire fame and money or self-satisfaction by sensational performances, often in productions without meaning—the opposite of play. It is even more obvious in sports, which can carry for so many the spirit of true play, but which in our day are becoming swallowed up in the atmosphere of big business. The players are of course truly playing when they put out all their skill and strength to win, thus reflecting archetypal conflicts. And there still remains in many great individual players and coaches the recognition that without the experience of defeat as well as the exhilaration of victory there can be no real meaning in play. But victory at all costs—secret drugging, violence, corruption, and greed—threatens all sports, and indeed all our activities that cease to be games but become competition for the satisfaction of any kind of demand of the ego. The enormous popularity of sports is a symptom of the deep yearning in all of us for the spirit of play. Through the enjoyment of such things we may discover at last that until our whole lives, whether working or at leisure, are infused by the joy and laughter of play for its own sake—never for the sake of gain—we are not truly alive at all. Work and play would then no longer be opposed to each other but at one in all the different aspects of our lives. Schiller said (again as quoted by Jung), "Man is only fully human when he is at play."

We may begin to intuit the nature of true play if we listen and listen again to the words of Sophia, the holy wisdom of the feminine in the Godhead. They are written in the Book of Wisdom (8:22-25) and are also the epistle for the celebration of the birth of Mary, the mother of God, in the Roman Catholic liturgy. Without this wisdom of Sophia there can be no Mary within us, women or men, to give birth to the divine, incarnate Child. The translation is from the Douai Bible. I quote extracts from the passage:

> The Lord possessed me from the beginning of his ways, before he made anything from the beginning. I was set up from eternity, and of old, before the earth was made. . . I was with him forming all things and was delighted every day, playing before him at all times, playing in the world; and my delight is to be with the children of men. Now, therefore, ye children, hear me. Blessed are they that keep my ways. Hear instruction and be wise and refuse it not. Blessed is the man that heareth me, and that watcheth daily at my gates and waiteth at the posts of my doors. He that shall find me shall find life, and shall have salvation from the Lord.

When Christ said, "Whosoever shall not receive the kingdom of God as a little Child, he shall not enter therein" (Mark 10: 15), he was speaking out of this feminine divine wisdom, affirming that beyond the essential "ethical phase," to use Jung's phrase, and beyond all the splendor and beauty of theology, of philosophy, of psychology and scientific research, beyond all the efforts of humankind to understand good and evil, matter and spirit, there still remains a gate through which we must pass if we are to find the ultimate freedom of "the kingdom of Heaven." It is the gateway to the spontaneous play, not childish but childlike, of the feminine spirit. Without it there never could have been and cannot ever be any creation that knows eternity again after the long journey of Return in the dimension of time. She is and always has been "playing in the world" in the sheer delight of the Fool and the Child hidden in every one of us. As we wait "at the posts of her doors" she may reveal herself to us: then indeed all work is transformed into play and play becomes the work that is contemplation, and we know the delight of being with the sons (and daughters) of men.

I was in the process of writing the above when, synchronistically, I received the notice of a seminar to be given by Adolf Guggenbühl-Craig in New York on "Aging." In the summary of his theme it is said that he suggests it is time to see aging as a process of becoming free: "The real archetypal image, the stimulating symbol for the aging would be, not the wise old man or woman, but the 'foolish' old man or woman"; then they would find freedom from all conventions and would not care if they show their deficiencies. They would be able to let go of all need to be wise and to do the right thing; they could admit now that they don't understand the world anymore. The archetype would be more accurately described as the Fool and the Child within us rather than as "foolish." The freedom of the Fool and the Child is never silly: it is Sophia "playing in the world."

Let us look at some characters created for us by very great storytellers and "explorers of darkness" in our literature—characters who awaken in us that kind of laughter that is beyond all analysis. Through these images we experience the wonder of that sense of humor which, breaking through the bonds of cause-and-effect thinking and superficial morality, touches the innocence of the Fool and the Child in us and brings with it compassion and love.

In Dickens' novel *Dombey and Son,* who can ever forget Mr. Toots? In our day he would have been labeled with some of those empty collective words—"handicapped," "retarded," "brain-damaged," etc.—and treated accordingly, but even today one feels he would have transcended all that. There are many comic characters in Dickens—some great like Toots; others, like Captain Cuttle in the same novel, who are mildly funny, though somewhat boring, and do not awaken that fundamental laughter at all. Why? Because Mr. Toots and his peers are wholly themselves as a small child is wholly him- or herself and have at the same time a strange kind of natural wisdom that cannot be defined. Mr. Toots, as G. K. Chesterton so beautifully said of him, "always got all the outside things wrong, but all the inside things right." His natural emotions are wholly involved in what he does and feels, but he always assures everyone that it is "of no consequence," as indeed he knows in the humility of his extraordinarily accurate sense of proportion. Susan Nipper, whom he eventually marries, says of him, "Immediately I see that innocent in the hall I burst out laughing first and then I choked."

The second immortal image, whom one hardly dares to approach, is Shakespeare's Sir John Falstaff. How can one speak of the essential innocence of the Fool in that fat, drunken, cowardly thief and deceiver? Yet it is there, miraculously there; and he inspires so much true laughter, so much love and delight, both among those who have been most injured by him in the play and in all those blessed with a true sense of humor who read and reread his story, that again we are left with a vision of wonder and delight beyond that final gateway into freedom. This miracle is of course absent from the Falstaff of *The Merry Wives of Windsor,* who is primarily a figure of farce: we may laugh at this Falstaff but we cannot love him. In *Henry IV* and *Henry V,* however, that kind of laughter disappears, and if we start judging his deplorable qualities we miss the point absolutely. He is as he is and retains that extraordinary divine quality through it all. He truly loves "sack," as he truly loves life. "If I had a thousand sons, the first humane principle I would teach them should be to forswear thin potations and to addict themselves to sack" *(Henry IV, Part II,* IV.3). On the rational level his long paean to "sack" is indeed nonsense, but on Falstaff's lips it is a gorgeous celebration of joy in life. Let us indeed forswear the thin potations that we so often give our souls to drink with dreary solemnity. Let it be noted also that we never see him actually drunk. He "misleads" the young prince indeed, though we somehow feel that Hal was able to become a much more whole person because of that "bad" company. For Falstaff creates laughter of the deepest kind all around him and there is no "why" about it. Even the Chief Justice, most reasonably rebuking him for his outrageous behavior, is unconsciously won over.

We feel the tragedy of his rejection, harsh, however necessary, by the Prince, now king; and in *Henry V* we are deeply moved by the account of his illness and death when he was nursed by Mistress Quickly—the woman whom he had almost ruined financially and who loved him nevertheless. "Nay, sure, he's not in hell: he's in Arthur's bosom if ever man went to Arthur's bosom. A' made a finer end and went away an it had been any christom child...." And Bardolph, his much abused servant, says, "Would I were with him whether in heaven or in hell!" (II.3) How splendid a tribute! Laughter and tears come together as we read this scene if we hear it with the sense of humor in which these two realities are always present.

Early in *Henry IV, Part II* Falstaff seems to recognize for a moment his extraordinary vocation as a kind of divine Fool: "The brain of this foolish-compounded clay, man, is not able to invent anything that tends to laughter, more than I invent or is invented on me: I am not only witty in myself, but the cause that wit is in other men." And later he surely has his values straight when, after the young sober Duke John of Lancaster has said pompously, "I, in my condition, shall better speak of you than you deserve," Falstaff says to himself, "I would you had but the wit: 'twere better than your dukedom. Good faith, this same young sober-blooded boy doth not love me; nor a man cannot make him laugh" (IV.3).

In our own time the voice of Christopher Alexander is being heard by more and more seekers. He has written and is writing of architecture, of building, as a way to the creation of wholeness in the individual and in the community; and he speaks the same truths as do all the other contemplatives through the ages. In a seminar of his on tape one can hear his belly-laugh and recognize it as of the same nature as that of Jung and of Charles Williams as described here—of the same nature as that which bubbles up with our tears as we meet and experience such characters as Toots and Falstaff. In *The Timeless Way of Building* Alexander writes about the long discipline (the ethical phase of the search for self-knowledge) that teaches us "the true relationship between ourselves and our surroundings." We come then at last to the perception which he calls "egoless" and then he says we may pass through

> the gate which leads you to the state of mind in which you live so close to your own heart that you no longer need a language (the old discipline) and it is utterly ordinary, it is what is in you already ... there is no skill required. It is only a question of whether you will allow yourself to be ordinary and to do what comes naturally to you, and what seems most sensible to your own heart, not to the images which false learning has coated on your mind.

When we will consent to be "utterly ordinary," to be simple instead of wise, then the "humors" will transform into that *sense* of humor that brings sheer delight in that ordinariness, in the joy of what *is*. Then our instinctive emotions, our moods, the "melancholic, choleric, sanguine or phlegmatic humors" will no longer possess us and project themselves around us in the unconscious. These projections always add to the weight that breeds a desperate need to create drama and excitement in the environment through the hidden greed that is a kind of "anti-play." Instead, in that perception of wonder that is the sense of humor, we can begin to play in the freedom and simplicity of the child. No longer will there be any need to strive after anything—especially not after the spiritual—because the spirit itself would be present in each moment. As the old monk who was the author of *The Cloud of Unknowing* in the fourteenth century wrote in his other little treatise, *The Book of Privy Counselling:* "[After the long work of learning to know your own sinfulness] stop thinking about what you are! Know only that you are what you are.... Remember that you possess an innate ability to know *that you are."* At this level the East and West with their different languages are at one. I quote from a book called *Be As You Are,* edited by David Godman,[9] about Sri Ramana Maharshi (1890–1950), that most simple and direct of Hindu sages, whose laughter and compassion reach us through his words and his silences. Answering a question, he said, "There is no greater mystery than this—that *being* the reality we seek to gain reality. We think there is something hiding our reality and that it must be destroyed before the reality is gained. It is ridiculous. A day will dawn when you will yourself laugh at your past efforts. That which will be on the day you laugh is also here and now." This is "the laughter at the heart of things": this is the Divine Comedy of Being.

GODDESS OF THE HEARTH

Laurens van der Post tells how he overheard a student at the Jungian Institute in Zürich saying to another student, "What is fire?" The reply was, "It is energy." "And I thought," continues van der Post, "dear Heaven, can we be as intellectual as all that? Surely fire is light in the dark, it is warmth against cold, it is security against the beast and the things that prowl by night. People no longer see the sun as a great source of light but as gases and sunspots. The great sun-within-themselves, their interaction between what goes on in the universe and themselves, is cut off.... Fire is just energy to us."[1]

When great symbols lose their content and their meaning for us, we are in danger of losing our souls. "This narrow, rational awareness that we have developed," says van der Post, "has cut us off from the image-making thing in us." So great is the pressure from the collective values of our time, however, that even for those of us who recognize this truth, there is need to struggle every day so that we may avoid falling into a subtle devaluation of all our efforts towards image-making. "What's the point?" says the voice of anima or animus; "Contemplating images is a waste of time. It changes nothing." On one level that is true; it changes nothing, for it opens the door to that which is eternal, bringing all the changing phenomena of our individual lives into relationship with the unchanging whole. But on the level of our limited consciousness, it is the only thing that changes *anything*. In particular, the contemplation of the symbol of fire, the experience in some measure of its infinity of meaning, is that which can establish the "interaction between ourselves and the universe," the rising of the "great sun within." For fire is the agent of transformation, and without it human beings would not have begun to emerge from the unconsciousness of the animal world.

For primitive man fire meant the living presence of the sun, the descent of the supreme spirit to earth, and with it came the capacity for conscious creation or destruction. Fire itself is forever the same in its essential nature, but it cannot burn at all here on earth without fuel, and it is the nature of the fuel with which a person feeds the fire, whether exterior or interior, that determines whether it will create or destroy. How exciting a thing it is when we see in imagination the first little flames kindled by the rubbing of sticks in the primeval forest! How exciting it is to remember at the same time the fire of the Spirit striking into the heart and womb of the mother of God, or the flames from above flickering on the heads of the apostles at Pentecost, and to *realize* that the great universal symbol of fire carries the same meaning at every level of consciousness! The fire descends to meet the fuel of earth and flames upward again towards its source.

The fire may kindle the wood of the hearth, or it may rage uncontrolled through the forest or the house; it may light the gentle wick of a candle or the tiny fuse that explodes a bomb; it may evoke the life-giving blaze of imagination, the warmth of tenderness and love, or the murderous emotions of anger and hate and lust. "The only hope or else despair lies in the *choice* of pyre or pyre," wrote T. S. Eliot.[2]

It is the crucial matter of the choice of fuel that is the subject of the *I Ching* hexagram 30,[3] which is the doubled trigram meaning *Fire*. It is called "The Clinging," directing attention to the fact that fire must cling to something in order to burn at all. The words of the Judgment are somewhat of a shock. "The Clinging. Perseverance furthers. It brings success. Care of the cow brings good fortune." The image of the cow is so remote from either fuel or fire, it seems, that we are bewildered. A footnote in the Baynes-Wilhelm translation points out that in the Parsee religion the worship of fire is also associated with the cow, so that it is not a purely Chinese image.

If we look a little deeper, however, we begin to see how true it is that the moment we cease to "care for the cow," the fire either goes out or rages out of control to our destruction. Ahura Mazda, god of light and wisdom in Zoroastrianism, was nourished on the milk of the cow when he came to earth. Only the particular essence of the feminine principle symbolized by the cow can maintain the steady flame of the inner light. For the cow means something more specific than simple motherhood. She stands in our imagination as an image of the slow, patient chewing of the cud which turns the grass of the earth into human food. Receiving the seed of the fiery bull, she conceives, but the milk which she produces for her young may also, if consciously drawn upon, provide nourishment not only for human beings, but even for the god incarnate himself. The cow is the passive, feminine heat of unremitting attention without which there can be no transformation by fire. The alchemist mixing his raw materials with superlative skill in his retort could have achieved nothing if he had not tended the fire underneath it day and night, so that it might not burn too high or too low. So also must the cook watch in her kitchen, the smith in his smithy, and, most earnestly of all, every person who seeks to transform the raw material of his or her life into the gold of consciousness. For if the fire goes out or burns too fiercely, it is very likely that he must begin all over again. It is only if we will drink daily of the milk of the "cow" within us that we can find strength for this. One word for this inner care of the cow is *rumination,* which is derived directly from the chewing of the cud.

There is no mention at all in the hexagram of the fiery bull. The message of the *I Ching* is to the "superior man," that is to say, in our language, to the conscious person—the person who has already recognized that the bull must be sacrificed. For the fire of which the hexagram speaks is the inner light, the great sun-within-ourselves, of which we can be fully aware only when the wild instinctive fire of the bull has been experienced, accepted, and transformed.

The bull appears again and again in antiquity as the sacrificial animal, for example in the Mithraic mysteries and in the original symbolism of the bullfight. The cow is not sacrificed, for her milk is necessary to the god, and she is therefore already sacred.

In the ox-herding pictures and poems of Zen, we see the wild bull gradually turning from black to white. First the herdsman must find the black bull; then he uses whip and lash, then a rope; then he is able to ride peacefully without bridle; at last the bull is free to roam harmlessly where he will—and now he is wholly white. The fire of indiscriminate emotion is fire from heaven like any other, burning to fulfill its nature through union with the fuel, the object of desire, but burning itself out without meaning, until through discipline, conscious watching, and acceptance, the change of fuel brings transformation and freedom. The bull is no longer black, unconscious affect; he is white, creative fire.

It is at this point that the *I Ching* warns us of danger, for the taming of the bull *may* be mere repression by a superficial, highly developed ego-consciousness. If the clarity that we have achieved turns to intellect uprooted from life and we forget the cow—if indeed we neglect the cow at any point along the way—then the fire "flames up, dies down, is thrown away," in the words of line 4. The commentary adds, "Clarity of mind has the same relation to life as fire has to wood. Fire clings to wood but also consumes it. Clarity of mind is rooted in life but can also consume it." This wisdom comes to us over three thousand years and is more urgently applicable today than ever before, for we are in danger indeed of a final flaming up, a dying, a throwing away of human life on earth precisely because of our neglect of the *cow.* Clarity of mind has become identical with intellect; because we so quickly forget or regard as unimportant the constant chewing of the green grass of the earth, the daily inner rumination that is the drawing of the milk of simple human kindness, the nourishment of the quiet heart.

Thus the whole course of a person's life depends on the nature of the fuel that day by day he or she feeds to the fire of being, either consciously or unconsciously. "We only live, only suspire, consumed by either fire or fire," said T. S. Eliot.[4] When the fuel is provided by an ego dominated by unconscious desire, the fire will be a straw fire, flaring up in emotional reactions, positive or negative, power drives, or intellectual ambitions, transforming nothing. Line 3 of the hexagram refers to this: "In the light of the setting sun men either beat the pot and sing or loudly bewail the approach of old age." Not only in the matter of old age do we do this. When we burn in this way, swinging from one opposite to the other, the cow is starving, forgotten, neglected, and slowly we are consumed, become meaningless, are "thrown away."

This is one of Eliot's two fires. What of the other? The spark of the creative imagination, the objective warmth of the heart, the flames of conscious suffering, and the white fire of the Spirit—all these will burn only if we will care for the cow. Cow's milk, cow's urine, and cow's dung all partake of the holiness of the cow in India. In glaring contrast to this, there is contempt in the West for this image. To call a woman a cow is an insult. Yet even here our unconscious knows better and it has thrown up into speech the exclamation "Holy cow!" I heard someone exclaim recently, "Holy cow! How the walls of Jericho have come tumbling down!" How right the strange juxtaposition of images was! Only after the long hard times of accepting and quietly chewing the cud of facts, of maintaining patience in the face of no visible results, does the trumpet sound and down come the walls of Jericho. The inner fire is lit, but it will burn with a steady light only so long as we feed it daily with the necessary fuel. In the story of Moses' life all this is very clear. The fire blazed up in his generous emotion of pity for the man beaten by the overseer; he fed it with an angry act, and it burned itself out in the destruction of the overseer's life. But Moses had learned the lesson. He went into the wilderness, and through the long years of exile, the quiet tending of the flocks, the finding of his bride, his feeling nature, he took care of the cow within. He was nourished by the "milk" of his patient waiting, and, when the time was ripe, the fire blazed up again; and out of the bush which burned and was *not* destroyed (for even the fire which does *not* consume must have fuel) he heard the voice of God. So the fire of his spirit was kindled, and all through his long life of devotion it burned steadily on the fuel of his accepted responsibility and his endurance, his unremitting care for his people. The fierce heat burned out in him all his ego-concern; it kept alive the pillar of fire by night; it turned aside the wrath of God. Only once did he fall and feed it with personal anger, identifying with the fire itself when he struck the rock, oblivious for that brief moment of the patient "cow" whose milk was his sustenance through those long years. This milk alone it is that ensures the burning which does not destroy and from which the voice of God speaks to a man or a woman.

The artist must similarly feed the burning fire of his vocation. The fuel of his art, the hard discipline and often agonizing work of making his vision incarnate, will soon be abandoned and the fire burn itself out if he will not "care for the cow," will not endure the dry periods when the flame of imagination seems totally extinct, will not learn the slow tempo of the cow, while in the passive feminine womb of the unconscious the seed matures. Blake is a shining example of an artist whose inner fire burned with such terrifying power that it threatened to consume him utterly and destroy his sanity. He was saved by his "care of the cow." He married a woman with whom, it seems, he was not passionately in love, but with her he was able to build a home rooted in the simple values of earth, and in it was lit the hearth fire of quiet day-by-day devotion. Thus he was nourished on the milk of human warmth and relatedness, and the fire was contained so that he could give enduring form to his burning visions.

By long years of caring for the cow the brightness is perpetuated, and in men like Blake, the great sun-within-themselves shines out into life and back from the four quarters of the world to the center of their being. They have achieved "interaction between themselves and the universe."

The *I Ching* speaks of the great man, but all of us, however small we may feel, can become aware to some degree of this brightness and can perpetuate this awareness. Our danger is more often that the fire of imagination will go out for lack of fuel than that it will blaze up and destroy us. All have somewhere buried away the capacity for image-making, and the little spark can be nursed into a blaze only if we will care for our cow. She must be milked without fail, morning and evening, or she will sicken and die. We must draw the milk and drink it; otherwise the patience that seeks out the right twigs to feed the flames will soon peter out, and under our conscious apathy, we will be feeding the destructive fires below. A cow cannot wait very long to be relieved of her milk. A farmer cannot say, "I am too busy today" or "I don't feel like it." But to modern men and women, these two phrases are a constant justification of neglect of the cow.

The feeding of the hearth fire is, of course, the special concern of woman. We think of the hearth as the center of the feeling life of the family, and its quality depends upon the mother—the mother in each of us whether we have physical children or no. Therefore it is startling at first when we remember that the Goddess of the Hearth in ancient Greece was Hestia, a virgin. Her Roman name was Vesta, and the sacred hearth fire of the city was tended by the Vestal Virgins. This has a profound meaning for us. The central warmth of a home will be a matter of fleeting emotions—blazing up, going out, overheating or underheating—unless the woman who tends the hearth fire is in touch with her virginity; unless she nourishes the fundamental feeling values from that part of herself which is "virgin" in the ancient sense of the word, for it originally meant "she who is one-in-herself." Philo of Alexandria said that when a virgin lay with a man she became a woman, but when God began to have intercourse with the soul, she who was woman became virgin again.

To the extent, then, that a woman has found herself as separate, one-in-herself, has freed her emotional life from possession and possessiveness, to this degree only can she bring unity to the family around the hearth. Even if she lives physically alone, the image holds. As she grows to this maturity of feeling she will tend the hearth fire day and night, as the Vestal Virgins tended the hearth fire of the city. The virginity of the Mother of God, which is so thin a concept when confined to the physical plane, takes on its full and overwhelmingly beautiful meaning when we begin to be aware of these things in our ordinary daily lives. No woman has found a true relationship with a man or the real meaning of motherhood until she has also to some degree found herself consciously as virgin—one-in-herself. We do well to remember at this point the symbol of the holy prostitute in the ancient mysteries of woman, for the conventional meaning of virginity as a refusal of sexual experience so easily creeps back into our thinking. The woman's giving of her body to "the stranger" in the temple brings home to us the strange paradoxical truth that a woman cannot become "virgin" in the conscious sense unless she is capable of a total giving of herself, body as well as soul. She must burn in the fires of instinct, and then be willing to give herself totally to "the stranger," that is, where her emotions are not involved, or perhaps, as Esther Harding has said, to do the hardest thing of all for the feminine psyche, to allow herself to love with her whole being someone from whom she knows she can expect no return, no fruition.

The experience of virginity is not a cold thing. It may be felt with a burning intensity at moments when the body is on fire with unfulfilled desire, provided one is consciously aware that this desire will, if we endure and contain it, consume the demands of our concupiscence, while proclaiming the beauty of instinct and its validity. An experience of this nature has a kind of cleanness and purity which is the essence of real virginity. These things she can only do when she begins to live the symbolic life—to enter the temple and become a prostitute therein. From it she emerges a virgin, and the hearth fire will burn wherever she may be and many will be warmed and strengthened thereby.

None of this, however, can possibly come about in her if she neglects her essential feminine cow-likeness. She must *produce* milk, not only drink it. Through all her experiences, from virgin to woman to virgin again, she must constantly digest the green grass of her earthly experience and give the milk of her feminine warmth to all who will draw it, not thrusting it at people, but simply letting it down at the touch of a milker's fingers.

Finally the fires of desire, of imagination, of the heart, all the lesser fires of our experience, bring us to the purging fire of sacrifice. Jung has said that in some traditions the cross is a symbol of fire, and that this may be due to the association with the rubbing of two sticks to produce fire. Primitives thought of these as masculine and feminine. They meet, and the rubbing, the friction between them, brings the fire of life to earth. The Christian cross is, of course, the great symbol of the fire of suffering. "Whosoever is near to me is near to the fire" is an apocryphal saying of Christ. There comes a time when it is no longer a question of tending fires, of finding fuel, but of becoming ourselves the fuel, walking open-eyed into the flames.

In our dreams we find images of all the different kinds of fuel that determine the nature of the fire in our lives, the direction of all our psychic energy. Dreams of fires burning and destroying indiscriminately will tell us of the raging of unacknowledged emotions in the unconscious; dreams of hearth fires lit in the wrong places or of furnaces in the basement, either with flames leaking out or stone cold, warn us to look to the "virginity" of our feelings; dreams of fire cooking food speak of the alchemical transforming process at work; and candles burning steadily awaken quiet devotion. We may see a light blazing in darkness, illuminating, bringing consciousness, or a fire on which burns a symbol of some old attitude to be sacrificed. Occasionally there comes a great dream of the fire into which we must voluntarily enter and give ourselves up.

Through "care of the cow" all these images may be "perpetuated" and experienced as daily reality. Then indeed the "great-sun-within" begins to rise and to illuminate the four quarters of the world, the four-fold wholeness of the individual person. So finally we may come to know "the condition of complete simplicity" of which T. S. Eliot speaks in *The Four Quartets* where "the fire and the rose are one."[5]

Notes

The Merchant of Venice

1 References are to act and scene.

Antony and Cleopatra

1 *The Meaning of Shakespeare,* vol. 2 (Chicago: University of Chicago Press, 1960), p. 208.

2 References are to act and scene.

3 *C. G. Jung Letters,* vol. 2, selected and edited by Gerhard Adler in collaboration with Aniela Jaffé (Bollingen Series; Princeton: Princeton University Press, 1953), p. 496.

4 Edinger in *American Nekyia,* Winter, 1976, p. 54. "Fate is everything that happens as a result of unconscious dynamisms—to the extent that one is conscious fate is changed into choice."

5 To quote again from *American Nekyia,* Summer, 1976: Edinger has been speaking of the instinct of self-preservation in nature and its equivalent in the psyche, that which preserves the integrity of our being, our urge to individuation. "It derives from the self and is experienced as a transpersonal power which transcends the ego. The man who sacrifices his own life rather than submit to an intolerable indignity is operating out of a supra personal dynamism. Symbolically he is acting out the 'will of God' who will not have the central value of the personality denied. It must be remembered, in reading these scenes, that for the pagan the inner and the outer were one thing. Christianity had not yet widely separated the psychic and the physical. Only a few philosophers were yet conscious enough to know that an outer 'intolerable indignity' is not necessarily a threat to the psychic integrity of being."

The Stranger Within

1 Dallas: Spring Publications, 1963.

2 Sir Laurens van der Post, *The Lost World of the Kalahari* (1977) and *The Heart of the Hunter* (1980), both published by Harcourt, Brace and Jovanovich.

3 Translations are from the Jerusalem Bible.

4 Shakespeare, *A Midsummer Night's Dream,* act IV, scene 1.

5 *Ibid.*

6 All quotes from "The Story of Baucis and Philemon" are from Ovid, *Metamorphoses,* translated by Rolf Humphries (Bloomington, Ind.: Indiana University Press, 1955).

Jacob and Esau

1 *Kaleidoscope: "The Way of Woman" and Other Essays* (New York: Parabola Books, 1992), Ch. 26.

The Laughter at the Heart of Things

[1] Barbara Hannah, *Jung, His Life and Work: A Biographical Memoir* (New York: G. P. Putnam's Sons, 1976).

[2] Charles Williams, *All Hallows' Eve* (New York: Farrar, Straus & Giroux, 1948).

[3] *Ibid.*

[4] *Ibid.*

[5] Laurens van der Post, *Jung and the Story of Our Time* (New York: Pantheon Books, 1975).

[6] C. G. Jung, *Letters, vol. 1* (Princeton: Princeton University Press, 1973).

[7] Van der Post, *op. cit.*

[8] Etty Hillesum, *An Interrupted Life* (New York: Washington Square Press Pocketbooks, 1985.)

[9] David Godman, ed., *Be As You Are: The Teachings of Sri Ramana Maharshi,* (London: Arkana Books Paperback, Routledge & Kegan Paul, 1985).

Goddess of the Hearth

[1] Laurens van der Post, *Patterns of Renewal,* Pendle Hill Pamphlet no. 121, 1962, p. 47.

[2] T. S. Eliot, *The Four Quartets* (London: Faber & Faber, 1944), p. 42.

[3] *I Ching,* Richard Wilhelm version, translated by Cary F. Baynes, Bollingen Series XIX (New York: Pantheon, 1967).

[4] Eliot, *The Four Quartets.*

[5] Ibid., p. 44.